HIGH ON THE DOWNS

High on the Downs

A Festschrift for Harry Guest

edited by
Tony Lopez

Shearsman Books

Published in the United Kingdom in 2012 by
Shearsman Books Ltd
50 Westons Hill Drive
Emersons Green
Bristol
BS16 7DF

Shearsman Books Ltd Registered Office
30–31 St. James Place, Mangotsfield, Bristol BS16 9JB
(this address not for correspondence)

ISBN 978-1-84861-223-5
First Edition

This selection copyright © Tony Lopez, 2012.

Upon publication copyright in the individual works printed here reverts to the individual authors, whose rights to be identified as the authors thereof have been asserted by them in accordance with the Copyrights, Designs and Patents Act of 1988.
All rights reserved.

Acknowledgements

Previously published poems and excerpts by Harry Guest
are reprinted here by permission of Anvil Press Poetry.

'Heritage and Peril' by Harry Guest was first published in a Japanese version by Niikuni Seiichi in *Asa*, 1970; the new English translation from the Japanese version printed here is by Andrew Houwen. Peter Greening's 'Review of A Puzzling Harvest' was first published in *London Magazine*, 2003.
Rupert M. Loydell's poem 'Boathouse, Early Morning' was first published in *Between Dark Dreams*, Acumen Publications, 1992.
John Mingay's review 'It's Hard to Hold the Past' was first published in *Stride* magazine, 2011.
William Oxley's poem 'Ecclesiastical Polity' first appeared in *The Interpreter's House*.

Contents

Editor's Preface	7
Harry Guest	9
Joan Bakewell	18
Michael Bakewell	21
Humphrey Burton	24
Jack Chalkley	25
Owen Davis	27
Peter Dent	28
William I. Elliott	30
Peter Finch	31
Chris Finn	33
John Flower	36
John Ford	40
Peter France	45
John Greening	51
John Hall	56
Christopher Hampton	57
David Hare	60
Lee Harwood	62
Jeremy Hilton	66
Andrew Houwen	68
Harry Guest / Andrew Houwen	74
Peter Jay	77
Peter Josyph	80
philip kuhn	82
Ann Leaney	84
Tony Lopez	86
Rupert M. Loydell	94
John Mingay	96
Bob Nash	102
William Oxley	104
Alasdair Paterson	107
Michael Power	109
Tim Rice	110

Anthony Rudolf	112
Lawrence Sail	116
Daniele Serafini	117
Martin Sorrell	120
Peter Southgate	123
Anne Stevenson	126
Chris Ward	128

Preface

> We have lived elsewhere. How otherwise explain
> the shock of recognition at the gap in the hedge,
> that day high on the downs when the sun led you
> to a place you knew though it was your first visit.
> Harry Guest, 'The Sixth Elegy'

These various tributes and memoirs for Harry Guest on his 80th birthday immediately show in what regard he is held amongst those who have known him as a poet, translator and teacher. It is clear that he has had a profound impact on many lives. I have known him for 35 years or so; we are of different generations, and I consider him to be the best of friends: good company, perceptive, funny, generous, tolerant, and true. Much as I enjoy his friendship and think of him as my particular friend (as many others surely do), I know that he is also a major literary artist whose best work is of permanent value in English poetry, and that he has written translations that extend our understanding and appreciation of European and Japanese literatures.

Harry's poetry began to be published in pamphlets and books in the 1960s with *Private View* (1962), *A Different Darkness* (1964), and his first Anvil collection *Arrangements* (1968). His early work is of the same era as the artists David Hockney, Peter Blake and R.B. Kitaj, who were concerned to present the complexity of lived experience in a new and vital manner, as directly as possible and without filler. Harry's poem 'Montage' from that time depicts just the same kind of contemporary reality, at once intimate and public, cultured, tender and sometimes violent, but also in thrall to the glamour of the movies.

> The lamp made your skin glow, at last
> naked underneath my kisses.
> . . .
> I lay with you on the rumpled bed,
> and talked about Axel Heyst, the paperback
> on the one table by the cheap wine,
> the tooth-mug stained a hard, irregular maroon,
> and the cigarette-packets in an alien script.

Months of preparation, briefing, prayers even.
For this.

The scene is sketched in quickly with precise and telling details in order to be undercut as the experience of a double agent, in some wartime scenario of sudden attacks and terrorism. The reference to Joseph Conrad's novel *Victory* feels personal and sets the mood. The maroon stain, the tooth-mug and the cigarette pack are the stuff of *films noirs* and Len Deighton novels; the intimate matter immediately creates emotional engagement, but the individuals are unknown and they remain unspecified. Their emotional lives may well be double like the clandestine political reality that they inhabit. This is a long way from the drab utility verse of The Movement and it shows a sense of daring and adventure to represent whatever life throws up.

Had Harry Guest worked along this line he would have been an interesting poet without doubt. But he went to Japan and assimilated another profoundly different aesthetic; he learnt Japanese and translated ancient and contemporary Japanese poetry. He used his knowledge of modern European languages to translate Ronsard, Baudelaire, Hugo, Verlaine, Rimbaud, Rilke, Brecht and others, and to really stretch his own writing capacity. One has to read the sequence 'Elegies' or later poems like 'On Golden Cap' or 'Comparisons' to understand the range and depth of his achievement as an original poet. This little book is the least we could do to show our appreciation of an extraordinary life and career very much in progress. It begins with some new poems and a translation by Harry Guest.

T.L.
2012

Harry Guest

To Lynn, December 28th, 1977

Like your nearness
no dark omen
reads exactly
months unseen so
darling until
night's blaze attains
real guesswork use
each star trembling

Into Out Of

Darkness to dawn. Coolness rising
with no fear of spread day. The known
panoply—magnolias, birdsong,
drifting mist, the lake: the moored bark
a given intimation, shore
invisible. Though, remembered,
one impulse of pure longing, a
childhood spent in prophesying
forgotten dreams, the absence of
love needing eventually
progression from nightmare to ease.
Gone splendour. The lawn, curving on,
leaves brighter borders, the colour
different—a green past recalling,
gestures to signal to gestures
recalling past green a different
colour, the borders brighter, leaves
on curving lawn, the splendour gone.
Ease to nightmare from progression

eventually needing love
of absence, the dreams forgotten:
prophesying in spent childhood
a longing pure of impulse, one
remembered though invisible
shore, intimation given. A
bark moored, the lake, the mist drifting,
birdsong, magnolia, panoply
known. The dayspread of fear? No. With
rising coolness, dawn to darkness.

My Parents

I woke up thinking they were still alive
and lay there for a moment smiling
blurry with sleep and planned
to share again with them a happy time
we'd spent together months past which
they couldn't have
                              yet picturing her smile
his caution their refuge our cohesion my
delight until truth's fist smashed through
the paper door of dream and I re-
orphaned now fell back on staring at
the dark
           him clapping when I then twelve
trod The Green Bridge of Wales to the end
and back high above swirling surf but her
anxiety
           in hospital my tonsils out
visiting-hours seven to half-past
she came each evening changing buses
three times both ways
                    he noticing
our neighbour's pregnant cat on the lawn

huskily divulged facts I didn't
understand found rather boring
soon forgot
           her on the wharf
when I'd come back from Paris
unexpectedly how did
she know
           his disappointment at
my poor degree her frown of worry once
I'd touched my aunt for dollars to buy a suit

him kissing her forehead in the morgue
which smelled of stale lilies
and four years later my having
to identify his corpse on the same slab
no flowers that time for he'd died alone

so many wanted and unwanted times
a patchwork world you can't control
old snapshots half-heard echoes veering past
blind alleys flickering deceptively

wake up like that into confusion
deaths denied forgotten shunned
hit back at mere reality and
                        and
                            and

      *   *   *

1. Shakespeare: *"Shall I compare thee…"*
2. Wordsworth: *"The world is too much with us…"*
3. Shelley: *Ozymandias*

1.	2.	3.
You	What	Lone
June's	we	place.
blue	see	Stone
noons?	*not*	face.
	seen.	
Your		Go
face	Seas—	near.
more	trees—	Show
grace.	mean	fear.
	more	
Must	tender	"My
die?	earned	"land!
Wrong!	for	"Bow!"
Trust my	splendour	
my	spurned.	Dry
song.		sand
		now.

Memory

for Jill and Annette

When I was three you taught me how to spell
Czechoslovakia backwards, a skill lost
With greying time but thankyou anyway.
Your presence despite absence like a shell
Picked up on a Welsh shore withholds the cost
Of love all three of us were glad to pay.

Ganymede's Dog
for Peter Jay, poet, translator, classicist, prince of publishers

Seeing his beautiful master borne strangely aloft
he barked out, looking up, a confusion of thought
come back this is silly dogs don't fly I can't follow up there
you know that what am I supposed to do come down
please

The sheep were grazing again, unconcerned.
Sudden shadow—whirr of great wings—boy's cry—
and they'd scattered till bird and young shepherd
were lost as a speck on the distance and life
re-began. Munch. Nice grass. Time for a piss.
Munch. Rest a bit. Remunch. Now's what matters.

The eagle, exhausted, dropped his burden
in the immortal lap and soared away crossly,
his duty done. The king of gods
dabbed the ragged claw-wounds, healing them,
then licked the boy's blood off his hands
smiling. Don't be afraid.

The dog would never know how his master
acquired a master who trained him to serve wine
and taught him perhaps more interesting tricks
until he grew too old. Then what?

Too hoarse to bark, he sat back, tongue lolling, tail still,
and gazed up at blue emptiness. He needs me.
He chose me from the litter. Drowned all
my brothers and sisters. Five of them. He wanted
me that's why. I need him too. What do I do now?
Come back.

Please.

Quatrain

He stands there lost in isolation so
A no-man's-land of wonder none would dare
Traverse fenced him that time or later though
The wind such as it was ruffled his hair

Cromlechs

for Tasha, Nichol and Sébastien

Each stone is shielded. This structure stands
the thinness of an ice-pane from the wind.

Erratic blocks in time. Alien
to conquest and the age of June.

This slope with cadences of further fields
inseparate from harvest.

These shapes, hacked out,
dragged here on heavy inches,
dwell still in their far tombs—
the spaces they were prised from
under tough heather.

Grey weight belonging otherwhere
lends them transience.

The landscape's curve alone
not interrupted by their being there
wages the passing storms.

The East

for Tony Frazer and Tony Lopez

Tunnel of spring
                  The plum-trees
blur vistas and the temple-roof
seems nearer on the lazy sky
of April
        Gong heard
behind flowered branches and a crisp
sequence of footfall on gravel
                        Steep
bridge climbing the carp-pond
                          Chill
lingering smell of incense
and the floorboards
worn black with worship
                      The gloom
condenses to a metal image
and five camellias strewn
dispute the further barriers of sight

The Quality of Mist

For Lee Harwood

Flood-roar from all around.
Soil trembles underfoot.
Wisps of grey enter the lungs.

A building where there wasn't one.
Elusive gleam that indicates
an area traversed. All at once

a clearing out of nowhere.
The few trees dripping.
A smell of conifers.

A gate creaks open. Footsteps
on stone. Which halt. A splash.
The silence quivers back to shape.

"Amour en mesme instant m'aiguillonne et m'arreste…"

Love can at the same moment goad and check,
Console and terrify, blaze up and freeze,
Pursue and flee, construct with care and wreck,
Crown me as victor, force me to my knees.

The plaything of the storm, tossed high, brought low,
I'm steered by Love erratically at will.
I feel secure awaiting the death-blow,
Believe I've won when I'm a loser still.

What pleased me once displeases me to-day.
I fall in love with her I don't desire.
Finding my heart's delight I'm led astray
And get entangled in protecting wire.
Knowing what can assist me in my plight
I move to act and fail to do what's right.

Philippe Desportes, *Les Amours d'Hippolyte XXVII*

Joan Bakewell

Where to start? Our friendship reaches back to our golden years. Will I remember them with accuracy, with nostalgia, with regret at lost times? Probably all three. Certain I am that they were golden.

I met Harry at Cambridge in the spring term of 1952, or is that right? The date eludes me, but not the memory. A tall gangling boy with dark-rimmed glasses and a habit of tipping his head to look through the upper half of the lenses, a habit that stayed with him through the years. We made a threesome, Harry, Michael Bakewell and myself, then Joan Rowlands. There were other friends around us, Jill, Jane, Maurice, Ronnie and, as students will, we would each interact with the others. But always there was a sense that we three had a core understanding: a mutual sympathy apart from others.

From the beginning Harry was a poet. He would stay with his calling for the next 60 years and it is with him still. He was editing poetry magazines while studying modern languages and his fluency has been manifest in his many wonderful translations. Fifty years later in my autobiography *The Centre of the Bed*, I refer to my adolescent love of Lamartine's poem 'Le Lac', and I asked Harry to translate one of its more romantic verses.

> Aimons donc, aimons donc! De l'heure fugitive,
> Hatons nous, jouissons!
> L'homme n'a point de port, le temps n'a point de rive:
> Il coule et nous passon!
>   —Lamartine

> Let's love each other then: enjoy before
> It is too late, each fleeting day.
> Man has no harbour, time no further shore—
> Hours drift by and we fade away.
>   —Guest

We were of a generation that defined itself as postwar. We were grateful to have survived what had been a vivid part of our young lives. The freedom from the threat that had engulfed our parents made us upbeat, optimistic, facing the future full of hope. We were thrilled by the creation of the Welfare State and absorbed its values into our bones. We regarded ourselves as privileged to have passed whatever exams it took to get us to our different colleges: Harry at Trinity Hall, Michael at Kings, and I myself at Newnham. We felt blessed to be there. We walked in sunlight together. And Harry wrote poems.

The friendships were to endure: Harry went to Paris and missed my wedding to Michael: but he wrote a beautiful Epithalamion:

> God bless your voyage, God prosper your own
> Richer delight and added exploration
> Of lands all lovers two by two have known.

Harry went to America: and we missed his wedding to Lynn, but rejoiced in spirit. It was to prove a blessed marriage, recorded in a steady and devoted stream of poems of love, their life together, their travels, their cats, and their happiness.

We have stayed close. Harry is godfather to my daughter Harriet—special poems mark her birth and her marriage. I am godmother to their son Nicholas. We have holidayed together, visited galleries, walked in the countryside, adored the cinema. When Harry was teaching at Felsted we visited for long weekends, enjoying sherry with fellow masters and walks in the muddied tracks of the Essex countryside. We met and got on well with his friends, the priest Peter Gamble, the painter Trevor Goodman, the composer and pianist Christopher Headington. When Harry and Lynn moved to Lancing College so did we: spending delicious weekends at their sunny home in Shoreham, before intrusive buildings cut off the lyrical view of the little port. At Lancing he had the distinction of teaching within the same year three pupils who were to become outstanding figures in the country's cultural life: David Hare, Tim Rice and Christopher Hampton. A hat-trick of talent.

Harry has travelled a good deal: I know because a cascade of postcards, dense with his small enthusiastic writing and crammed with nuggets of cultural news, has, over decades, poured through the letter box. Iceland, Peru, Canada, Japan… And always there are the poems. They are infused with a lyrical beauty and freshness that spring from his continuing engagement with the things he loves; his family, landscapes,

Joan Bakewell

the natural world in all its range and mystery. Michael and I were the dedicatees of 1970 volume of poems: *The Cutting-Room*. Later, my company The Drama House was to commission from Harry a poem for an Easter series we made for BBC Television. Our friendship has been laced through with poems. And I like to think that something of our lives, separate but close; have been part of all that informs the writing.

What makes a friendship endure so long? Our paths have not been the same: Harry has had a long and distinguished career as a teacher, finally in Exeter where in recent years he has added teaching Japanese to his other languages. He is currently lending support to a grandson obsessed with all things Japanese. I, in contrast, have moved in a wayward fashion across many reaches of the media world. But we have met regularly down the years in the true and safe knowledge of a friendship rooted in the same values, nourished by the love of ideas, and flourishing against the same cultural landscape. Our meetings are still voluble with opinions on everything from educational theory to the latest show at the Wallace Collection, from Damien Hirst to this year's Bayreuth Festival. We can disagree strongly without malice or hurt. I once asked Harry—a devout Christian throughout his life—whether in his view when we die he would go to Heaven and I, a non-believer, would not. He smiled ruefully. "Well, it's not really the right question to be asking." But I persisted: it was the start of a long discussion from which we both, I hope, gained insights.

As I grow older I have come to cherish friendship more than ever. Unlike the vagaries of careers and the unreliability of money, friendship remains secure and true. It is a gift Harry has brought into my life.

Michael Bakewell

Harry Guest: A Personal Memoir

Harry Guest and I met in a Chinese brothel in 1951. It was our first term at Cambridge and we had both been cast in one of those short plays put on by university drama societies to spot potential new talent. I played a languid, world-weary young Englishman while Harry was the lively and loquacious brothel servant. He had a much better time of it than I did and certainly got the laughs. One of his lines—You like our Chinese New Year?—has remained a catch-phrase between us for what is now over sixty years.

After that we started to meet every day. For me, having arrived in Cambridge after two years national service in the RAF where conversation had been distinctly unforthcoming, meeting Harry was like a great breath of fresh air. Not for him the kind of *Brideshead* disdain for university life, a pose adopted by so many in their first year at the time. He was there to enjoy every moment. His excitement was immediately contagious and his enthusiasms coloured everything he did. We would talk endlessly about art and literature in his rooms at Trinity Hall, or in mine at Kings, sometimes wandering along the Backs. Over omelettes at Lucy's, or a curry at the Taj we exchanged views about the writers whose works we admired or the paintings we loved. The Fitzwilliam was a regular haunt as was the Rex Cinema, famously managed by Leslie Halliwell and showing such classics as *Citizen Kane* and *Destry Rides Again*.

Our passion for music was another great bond between us, although, as far as I can remember neither of us had a radio or a gramophone in Cambridge. What I did have in my rooms at Kings, for reasons unknown to me, was an upright piano, which Harry found irresistible. Often he would play on late into the evening and I would eventually have to bundle him out so that I could finish some long overdue essay. The one thing we never discussed in all our time there was politics. I don't think it was a particularly conscious decision. It simply was something that did not concern us. Of course we talked a great deal about poetry and he showed me his poems. I was struck by their immediacy and depth, recognising in them, even on that first reading, the work of a true poet and his total commitment to his craft.

Now and again we would have an expedition to London. On one memorable occasion we went to a celebration of the tenth anniversary of the magazine *Adam* hosted by its editor Miron Grindea. It was introduced in a very rambling fashion by Bertrand Russell followed by contributions from various scions of the literary world. What made the evening for us was our encounter in the cloakroom with T.S. Eliot who appeared to be about to go off with my raincoat. I falteringly endeavoured to point this out to him while Harry, superbly self-assured and determined to make the most of the opportunity, asked how his new play—I think it must have been *The Confidential Clerk*—was coming along. The great man was modestly non-committal but Harry had done what, in those days, I would never have dared to do, he had initiated conversation with a legend.

In his second year, he founded, together with contemporaries Michael Podro and Ronald Hayman, a literary magazine, *Chequer*, designed to provide a forum for new writing and poetry in Cambridge. There have been dozens, possibly hundreds, of short-lived undergraduate magazines over the years but *Chequer* had quality and survived for eleven issues—something of a record in Cambridge—publishing among other things poems by Thom Gunn, Ted Hughes and Sylvia Plath and of course by Harry himself. He believed absolutely that new writers deserved a hearing and should be given the chance of a platform for their work.

A typical example of this, by no means universal, generosity of spirit came in 1953 when The Young Writers' Drama Group launched a playwriting competition which was won by Jennifer Petty's play, *The House*. When no one showed the least interest in performing it, Harry was incensed. Considering this to be outrageously unfair, he decided to put the play on himself. He hired a hall, assembled a cast from among his friends, found a set designer, organised advertising and a printer for the programmes. The play proved to be a success, but without Harry's support it would never have got off the ground.

When we went down from Cambridge in 1954 we were resolved to see one another as often as we could. It was easy enough when we could get together in London or at Harry's home in Broadstairs or when he was teaching at Felsted or Lancing. But, inevitably, with our lives going in different directions there were times when we couldn't meet at all. But Harry is a great letter-writer which was fortunate since I am a hopeless correspondent. What kept our friendship very much alive during those years he spent in Japan and gave it an unbroken continuity were his letters, always full of news and highly entertaining, they brimmed over with all the sparkle and warmth of his conversation. I particularly remember a letter in which he described his attempts to carry on teaching a class in the middle of an earthquake. When he came back to England, it was, of course, as if he had never been away but had slipped outside for a moment. We simply picked up the conversation where we had left off and the conversation still goes on.

What for me particularly characterises Harry, both in his work and in his life, is his determination to achieve all the goals he has set himself. There are not many about to be octogenarians who continue to seek new mountains to climb and actually make it to the summit but he is one of them.

Salutations dear Harry.

Humphrey Burton

I have no specific memory with which to regale Harry on the occasion of his Big 8 (I celebrated my own last year with a five-concert weekend of favourite music by Schubert) but I retain very pleasant *feelings* about the six months we shared as post-graduate students in Paris, January–June 1955. We both loved music and would have heard string quartets together (the Amadeus came to play Britten, I remember) and sat at the feet of Pierre Boulez for his Sunday morning Domaine Musicale events at the theatre in the Champs-Elysées where he served as music director for Jean-Louis Barrault's acting company. We would have seen members of the Pitoeff Family doing Chekhov in Montmartre and revelled in the success of Joan Littlewood's Theatre Workshop, who took Paris by storm that year with Volpone and Arden of Faversham. We would have gone on suburban picnics together to Ville d'Avray and met in the rue Visconti workshop of my friend Florence Jonquières, a weaver whose father printed special editions, exquisitely produced, of books by eminent luminaries of the Parisian literary establishment such as Jean Cocteau. Since we were both music buffs, Harry must often have been present when our group of friends, French and Swiss girls and an English oboist named Maurice Checker, played over and over again our favourite recording, the Concerto Grosso No 1 for strings and piano by Ernest Bloch. Perhaps Harry also attended the concert of piano duet music my Swiss girlfriend Claudine Effront and I gave at the end of my Parisian séjour in her landlady's drawing room, a handsome parlour, 17, Ave de Prony, in the XVIIth arrondisement. We were very hard up and for lunch would sometimes eat nothing more than the bread and mustard provided free at the Cité Universitaire. But it was a happy time and Harry taught me the importance of being positive, enthusiastic and cheerful.

Jack Chalkley

Tribute to HBG

Unlike Robin Reeve, another great mentor of mine, Harry Guest was barely my teacher at Lancing College, where he joined the staff in my second term and left at the end of my last. Yet I sense I owe my love for, and association with France, more to him than anyone else.

For a while I knew him only as the bachelor master who lived upstairs in Field's (my house), who moved with a rather rapid, asymmetrical gait, and whose intense diction was accompanied by expansive gestures, with large downward sweeps of the hand and blows to the brow; these widely adopted (and sometimes lampooned), by significant figures senior to me, among them the future playwrights, H. and H.

He taught me for half a term early in 1963 when, having just scraped through my "O" level re-takes, I was placed in his English set. He was obliged to try and take me through *Antony and Cleopatra* and *The Duchess of Malfi*, until my tutors decided—quite rightly—that two A-levels, not three, was absolutely enough for a rather immature 15-year to be facing in exams due to be taken little more than a year later.

Then, perhaps six months after that, there was a brief and mysterious period of further instruction (some kind of compensation or rescue scheme for those stuck with taking Latin and Greek, or kept on a restricted diet of natural science), when for a few weeks Harry taught a very assorted class of us a little twentieth-century French literature: Collette's *La seconde* (repeated reference to the imagery of ripeness), and Jacques Prévert's verse collection *Paroles* (careful explanation of the meaning of "connerie" in the lines "Oh Barbara / Quelle connerie la guerre", and so why the French preferred to speak of Sean Connery as 007). We were issued these texts in *Livre de Poche* editions, certainly the first French paperbacks that had fallen into my hands, and pretty exotic; the titles upside down on the spines, the covers shinier and more fragile than those of the handful of 3/6 orange Penguins that filled the shelves of my alley in the Field's houseroom.

Spared the agonies of the examination syllabus, I learnt French Civilization from him, not as a subject but as an aspiration, veiled but enticing: a highly desirable, and almost attainable, second identity. The France he offered was one stripped of geography, and largely of history. It definitely was not the holiday destination already familiar to me from visits to the châteaux of Chambord and Azay-le-Rideau, and from sweltering drives against the clock with my parents and sister back to channel ports through *la France du sol*. The France he offered was *la France des idées*, a cultural paradise, a place of thought and feeling, and passion and drama; of poets and singers and film directors, where Edith Piaf might die one week and Jean Cocteau the next, but nobody be taken in by this. They lived on.

Cocteau! Phrases from Harry's book of poems, *A Different Darkness*, are still with me, even though I mislaid my copy thirty years ago. "You played your death with cigarette smoke/And centaurs carried you away… A whiff of jazz … Now you are with Orpheus and the Chevaliers". Somewhere else in that volume came the phrase "Bartók on the pick-up". This was viewed as a bit "pseud" by my contemporaries, but I was myself terribly impressed as an eighteen-year-old, with pretensions to advanced taste in classical music, when Harry seized an A-level music paper and excitedly identified the unseen musical passage as the second subject of the first movement of Bartók's Concerto for Orchestra. This was possibly the last time I enjoyed his company, and I had known nothing of this interest of his.

I remember him, along with my distinguished history teacher, as the kindest and sanest of a small and distinguished band of radical figures at Lancing, less of the political left than of the intellectual heights. He was energetic. He was enthusiastic. He was restless. These were not regarded universally as desirable qualities among the Lancing teaching cadres. But perhaps of particular importance to me was that he did adventurous things, things which other teachers didn't do, like publish poetry, marry a beautiful American lady, and leave the sanctuary of the school to work in Japan…

Since when, Harry, no contact! What good fortune, though, to find myself through the attentiveness of my brother-in-law in a position to be writing something now!

Owen Davis

Back in Japan
for Harry Guest

Early April
And I'm back
In Japan.

Sunday morning
On a quiet street.

One moment at a time,
The blossoms fall.

A little girl in red
Waits on the white pavement.
Her eyes bright with expectancy.

Through black branches,
Here it comes.
The merriest cherry-blossom ever
To fall.

She dashes for it,
Arms outstretched,
Hands cupped.

And misses!
And misses two more.

Oh, I wish Harry were here
To watch her fail so joyfully.

Peter Dent

More Table Talk
for Harry Guest

It is counterfeit's genius to update the status quo   her model
of anxiety once more catches life in the round   look lively she
says   there is no book like an old book   keeping her word

Says someone vertigo goes green at the point of departure
it's like italics to look both ways then slope off says another
'to ruminate'   i.e. to load a vessel beyond its planned capacity

Or not   time's as temperamental as a penny's dreadful   all
you can assemble out of the kit of *A Life* is the kissing cousin
of an afternoon replete with disorder   Socrates wrote nothing

Never use words like 'symbolism' without prior consent   I've
been there and drawn the fever   a charcoal base will support
paintings no less occult than their subject   eyes whited out

I can't see the business lasting   a coalition has it in for itself
and everyone in particular   excuse please the entropic and
the double function of hard bonding and render asunder

It's bolted on to the rule book   a 'serious conviction' is all you
need and may be effectively discharged   like anything nature
has evolved for the purposes of pleasure   aren't we baroque!

Fancy rituals go with undecorated walls   contemporary
shortcomings throw off even the most pleasing of prospects
nothing you'd want to thumb through   to keep Britain clean

In the footsteps of Pyrrhon of Elis dodging this and every other
conviction   eyes focused enough to see nothing itself has an
edge   boulders in the foothills   the whole world in a spin

Towards an English Poem
after Harry Guest's 'English Poems'

Tell me then

about the colour
of the sun
in memories like this

if you make it back

checking on wear and tear
the weather a cast
of thousands brought

to bear   that variously

distant stream
things meant to matter?
striking a syllable or two

into the heart of who

we were   a late sun
paler as we saw it
like yesterday

turning in its gold

William I. Elliott

For Harry at Eighty

-i-
In the beginning were: the Word,
Logogram, hieroglyph and rune,
Smoked words of the Chippewa,
Love writ large by high pilots
And love signed by dexterous fingers—
All these were your predecessors, Harry,
None more eloquent than yours.

ENCAGED
-ii-
Logos talionis encaged,
The tamer knows what words can do:
Strip the skin of him
Down to the bone.
He knows. But in he goes,
With a whip and a stool.

-iii-
What
Transpires in the rear-end of a firefly,
Transpires in algae phosphorescent on the ocean floor,
Transpires in the prismatic fracturing of red to yellow,
Transpires in eyes opalescent in love,
Transpires in the shot sparks of short circuiting,
Transpires in the cracking of knuckles, of lightning,
Transpires, too, in your swarm of words chased and chaste.
The wary do well to wear goggles.

Peter Finch

Pursuing
For Harry Guest at 80

evidence bonfires water
oblivion entity landfall
fog lunatics time
hot knowing concentration
stillness resembling theoretic
gossip plastic remains
islands irregularity engulfed
terror notes craving
disintoxication filling catch
visitor skin brush
enigma alien maroon
vengeances terrorist flowers
levelled pathos blues
unravelling retreat wet
pyre acquiescence denial

the the the
the the the
the the the
the the the
the the the

the a the the the the
poem brush prescient
perfect tragedy pyjamas
flower absent contact
bronze light chocolate-box
noon frivolity ambiguous
injustice K.488 weed
irreverent myopic viewer
tea death antiseptic
nonchalant calm garbled
gesturing Samuel Beckett
gag asymmetric triumph
neglect uncarpeted thrice

ash   augury   revelation
tangible   scalpel   analysis
zen   index   apple
tones   swallow   fire
electric   fumble   unwoundable
a any   and   ack-ack
illuminated   bombs
despite   escalate   laziness
critically   set out   sugar bowls

Juxtaposition of *Arrangements* with *So Far*
juxtaposition of *Some Times* with *PMP No 16*
Juxtaposition of *The Cutting-Room* with *Coming to Terms*
Juxtaposition of *A House Against the something* with *Post-War* illegible
    on my copy
Juxtaposition of *Lost Pictures* with *The House Against The Night*
Juxtaposition of *A Puzzling Harvest* with *Comparisons and Conversions*
Juxtaposition of *PMP No 16* with *So Far* (one customer review)
Juxtaposition of *Lost Pictures* with *The Cutting-Room*
Juxtaposition of *The Cutting Room* with *Lost Pictures*
Juxtaposition of *Sometimes* with *Time After Time*
Juxtaposition of *The Cutting-Room* with *Mallarmé*
Juxtaposition of *Comparisons and Conversions* with *Arrangements*

atmospherics   without   pallor
crouched   overlapping   younger
ought   tiny   turf
intricacy   elation   enigma

mahogany   grey   Fiat
factory   yellow   gathering
drips   rock   rock
pursued   wrinkle   tranquillity

meanings   ripple
all ideas are ice
joy   canticles   eternity

Seventy-six lines concluding with the title
(now edited down to sixty-eight)
start again at the beginning

Chris Finn

Harry Guest

I worked with Harry for about twenty years. We were common-room colleagues and fellow wanderers in that particular wilderness. One of Harry's favourite works is Evelyn Waugh's *Scott-King's Modern Europe*, in which the classics teacher Scott-King, while working on a passage from Thucydides with the "lower school", says that it has been described as "tolling like a great bell", to which the immediate response from his pupils is the cry "The bell? Did you say it was the bell, Sir?" It was sometimes like that, with the sound in the background of "the strident tones of Griggs, the civics master, extolling the Tolpuddle martyrs". Griggs, by the way, had said to his pupils that "it's a pure waste of our time learning classics." Harry was always amused by and sympathetic to Paul Pennyfeather's teaching method where he offered "a prize of half a crown for the longest essay, irrespective of any possible merit". But during all this labour (and he always says he enjoyed teaching) his daily presence enriched my life, as well as the lives of many people around him. It was wonderful to have someone there who could share one's enthusiasms, and he introduced me to many writers and artists whose work is now a central part of my consciousness. It was Harry who first got me to read *Catch 22* (a long time ago), which I now regard as the last great masterpiece in the English language (though Harry would favour *Omeros*). He also discovered Eça de Queiroz and passed his enthusiasm on to me and recommended many Edith Wharton novels that I have relished. He loves Blake, Conrad, Wagner, Haydn, Shostakovich, Britten, Janáček, Balzac, Rimbaud, Verlaine, Hugo, Proust, Rothko. But his tastes are manifold and he is open to new ideas and forms at all times. I don't know if the influences ever worked the other way and if I was ever able to offer him ideas, but I do remember telling him about the unnoticed comet in Dyce's *Pegwell Bay*, which led to his poem "William Dyce: Pegwell Bay, Kent", in *Coming to Terms* (1994)

His attitudes to the modern world, or at least to the modern educational world, are less than enthusiastic. His wonderful poem 'Texting, Texting' is a sharp response to the degradation of language and standards of orderly discourse in the present, and he has watched with regret and perhaps fury as universities have pandered to the feeble excuses of modernity, reducing their demands on students and citing "relevance" as the prime criterion of intellectual regard. Perhaps the world was always like this, but Harry feels very acutely the way that the value of learning has been increasingly dismissed or described only in lip-service terms. Those of us who live here in Exeter feel a sinking of the heart at the reminder in the University Library that "The Forum is coming!"

He has his blind spots. He can only see the absurdity in ballet—without being troubled by the equal absurdity of opera. I tried to get him to read some of the early Scott, but unfortunate schooldays experiences, I think, made it impossible for him to contemplate. There is something of the Luddite about him, but perhaps that is unfair; his occasional technological ineptitude is quite unstudied and he has a firm conviction that today's modish wizardry is tomorrow's science-museum exhibit.

For nearly forty years my wife and I have been welcomed at Harry and Lynn's house, from which it has often proved impossible to escape sober, such is the richness of their hospitality. He continues to be a great favourite with the wives because of his quite unselfconscious gentlemanliness and his genuine interest in what others have to say. I have seen him sitting at the dinner table and completely forgetting to eat his own dinner, so absorbed is he in talking to whoever is sitting next to him and listening to what he or she has to say. The house is a delight, filled as it is with prints and mementoes from their years in Japan.

We have also been walking companions on many occasions, covering sections of the South West Coast Path as well as parts of Dartmoor and Exmoor. A particular favourite of his is the section of coast between Hartland Quay and Morwenstow and I often accompanied him when he took school groups there in the summer. Landscape is a true passion for him and living in Devon has allowed him to indulge it endlessly. A few years ago we walked a magnificent section of the Pennine Way, over Cross Fell. We stayed at Garrigill, Dufton (in the Youth Hostel which he very much disliked) and Middleton in Teesdale. I can particularly remember Harry walking down from the high moors towards Dufton, singing something from *Die Schöne Müllerin*.

When he retired from the classroom I was given the privilege of speaking his eulogy at the farewell dinner, and I remember that I said at the time that I felt he was the model of the well-adjusted and contented man, mainly because I can hardly remember an occasion on which he was manifestly unhappy (barring the night at the Dufton Youth Hostel). He remains immensely valued by his friends and colleagues, both for his brilliance and for his personal charm and generosity of spirit. In many ways my life would have been very different if I had never met him and he remains one of my closest friends. Last November he gave a reading of poems from his most recent collection, *Some Times*, where the whole audience must have been struck by the affection and respect with which he was regarded by everyone there. I feel endlessly privileged to have known him for so long.

John Flower

From Solutré, with Love…

Not so very long ago during one of those occasions when you realize you simply have too many books and papers and that the time has come to throw some out, I came across (folded inside André Gide's novel, *Les Faux-Monnayeurs*) an announcement of a "Day School" run by the University of Exeter's Department of French on 27 October 1988 in Reed Hall, in those days the Staff club. The theme was 'Words and their Illustration' and there were four invited speakers; I was one and so too was Harry Guest, described as a "poet and translator of poetry." Harry and I shared the afternoon session, it seems, and while I have to confess that I have no memory of the occasion I am sure that by then Harry and I must have known one another well.

The beginnings of our friendship a decade earlier had not been auspicious, however. Knowing I was about to take up a post at the University of Exeter in 1977, a former colleague said: "You must look out for Harry Guest, he teaches French at Exeter School." After we had arrived my then wife, Isabel, initially taught languages for a while at St Wilfred's School and soon found herself involved with pupil exchanges and school visits to France and Germany. An evening get-together for staff and spouses with colleagues from Exeter School was arranged and I dutifully attended. Here indeed was Harry. "You must be Harry Guest," I said, an opening which prompted a cold, almost dismissive response and it was clear that I should move on. (Harry claims to have forgotten this incident!) How, when and where our paths crossed after that first meeting I am not sure, but clearly they did—maybe in the Northcott Theatre bar, at concerts usually in the Barnfield theatre or the university's Great Hall where the Dartington String Quartet as resident musicians gave lunchtime performances, and no doubt during other student Open Days at the University—and we began to talk to one another civilly and even with pleasure.

Quite quickly I discovered something of Harry's background, activities and skills: Cambridge, a thesis on Mallarmé at the Sorbonne in Paris, Felsted School, Lancing College, Yokohama University Japan (where he spent six years) and Exeter School. What quickly became evident as well was his impressive competence in languages (French, German, Italian... and Japanese). Eventually he invited me to talk to his sixth-form pupils about their A-level work; their knowledge and sensitivity to the texts they were studying (at a time when literary texts still counted as worthy of study) was a tribute to their teacher for whom they clearly had admiration and respect. (Quite what Harry was like as a disciplinarian in the classroom I have difficulty in imagining, but perhaps his presence was enough.) It was not long either before Harry graced the Queen's Building at the University to read from his own work and to introduce discussions centred on the problems of translation. I recall distinctly that what struck the students was Harry's totally modest attitude and his unpretentious style of reading, and their appreciation was generous.

On the social front mutual invitations to drinks or dinner were soon in order. In fact Harry and Lynn nobly agreed to come one evening when we were hosting one of the University's Vice-Chancellors and his wife. But it was also thanks to completely informal visits that we became close. Most of these were at Alexandra Terrace where I would sometimes call well on into the evening with Smith, my Labrador of some size and character, who was fondly greeted, even if the cats decided not to stay with us, and where sherry or coffee was always instantly offered. Then, as now, Alexandra Terrace was a kind of cultural oasis—paintings, books in all languages, records, music on the piano... and talk.

After I had left Exeter for the delights of another cathedral town, Canterbury, and one of the so-called "new universities" created in the 1960s, I was delighted to invite Harry to lecture and share in seminars where he was no less warmly appreciated by my students and my new colleagues. Having Harry stay was also a pleasure not just for Julia, my wife, and myself but for Solutré our dog as well. Harry still recalls how this energetic bundle of black Schiperke mischief rifled through his bag to steal his hairbrush and promptly raced around the house refusing to give it to anybody!

Having become familiar with much of Harry's work over the years I have been increasingly moved by it. He has published over twenty books, primarily collections of poetry and three novels, the latter being in many respects autobiographical. As a poet Harry has the enviable gift of creating carefully crafted verse which at the same time prompts a deep emotional response. There can be no better illustration of his skills than *Versions* (1999). Written over more than twenty years the poems in this small volume are indeed "versions"—more than translations which Harry once described as "a subjective stab at the impossible"—of poems by eighteen of Europe's most demanding writers: Baudelaire, Rilke, Mallarmé or Hofmannsthal, for example. Equally rewarding are his translations of the thirty-three sonnets composed and memorized by Jean Cassou during his three-month imprisonment at the hands of the Vichy police in 1941-42, early in the Nazi Occupation of France, and eventually published by the clandestine Éditions de Minuit in 1944. What marks both books is the way Harry has succeeded in capturing the emotional and psychological tensions (and in the first of these volumes sometimes the humour) which pervade these poems but also maintains their structural rigour, especially that of the sonnet. And if further evidence were needed of Harry's subtle response to another language we only have to turn to *The Distance, The Shadows* (first published in 1981), his translations of a wide selection of poems by Victor Hugo, acknowledged by one reviewer as "uncanny" for the way they capture the tone and emotion of the original.

Harry is a consummate technician. Like some of the poets he so much admires he also experiments with the shape and style of his verse—the length of line, the rhyme schemes, a form of poetic prose, the lay-out on the page which has a direct effect on our reading. Foreign influences are there; the Japanese haiku is an obvious example but there are gestures as well to the late nineteenth- and early twentieth-century French poets, especially to Verlaine, Mallarmé and Apollinaire.

Impressive as this aspect of his verse is, however, I remain like most I imagine more moved by its content. Some of it is directly inspired by and dedicated to family and friends, living and dead; some contains hidden allusions to a very personal, even intimate past, to places visited, to meaningful events or the experience of foreign countries and cultures. But much stems and grows, like all good poetry, from the recording of a detail, "a tiny/ pond/flanked by a miniature/rock/ or/two"; "red grapes glued together"; flaked frescoes; a hawk; "Cold yellow afternoon"; "high white rain"… The list is endless. When Harry published *A Puzzling Harvest, 1955-2000,* his collected poems, in 2002 (despite being encouraged to do so by his publisher he admitted to having jettisoned only two!) I was familiar with many but I still found myself laughing aloud at some and in tears at others. The title, however, puzzled me; while harvest suggests fruition or fulfilment, much of

Harry's work, and especially that of the last thirty years, carries with it a sense of something not yet finished or not quite achieved. *Lost and Found, Lost Pictures, Coming to Terms, So Far, Some Times,* are titles which, for me at least, all hint at a past that rises to the surface but is accompanied by an awareness that much remains—a harvest which strangely lacks something. Whether Tom in *Time after Time* had a foresight that will turn out to be justified remains to be seen: "Actually I'm writing another novel," he says to Meirion, "I think of it as a sort of oblique and dishonest autobiography."

In addition to this wealth of imaginative work Harry has ventured into cultural guides with the *Traveller's Literary Guide to Japan* (1994), language instruction with *Mastering Japanese* (1989), reflections on art, literature and music in *The Artist on the Artist* (2000) and has reviewed for the *Journal of European Studies*.

By any standards Harry's achievement over nearly half a century demands respect and admiration, but it is the man behind it all who really matters. Every so often, if you are fortunate or are privileged, you meet someone who seems a to be a person for whom culture still deeply counts, someone for whom certain aspects of the contemporary world seem either to have been ignored or are simply irrelevant, unnecessary and probably wrong. This does not mean that they despise or turn their back on what that world has to offer, or indeed what is necessary for any kind of reasonably civilized existence. Such a person (to me at least) is Harry. Harry is a man for whom the pen remains preferable to the word processor; for whom the library is a place where books are kept and read rather than computers; for whom the motor-car is a necessary evil. He is a man with huge enthusiasms, a seemingly unquenchable thirst for art, literature, music and photography but who has as well a passionate interest in the natural world so beautifully exemplified by his nearby Dartmoor on which he has tramped hundreds of miles.

John Ford

A Note on Harry Guest's Poetry

In his poem 'On the Prescellies, June', Harry Guest writes:

> The most difficult thing
> is to stand on the spur
> while a late afternoon
> unfolds the haze or strikes
> the distant lines of hay
> and omit nothing, no
> note fallen from the high
> lark, no grey lamb bleating,
> no tang on the faint wind
> of clover, the day's warmth,
> salt and sheep's dung nor yet
> the open taste of air
> that has picked up nothing.

Surmounting this difficulty, if not impossibility, is at the core of much great poetry, and certainly of Harry's, and it is wonderful how successful he is in doing so. The rest of this poem, the whole poem in fact, is an appreciation of what one can see from one of the most striking viewpoints in west Wales. I myself have walked in this area, and his poem is very effective in bringing back to me what I felt and saw when I was there. This sort of subject has often been treated by poets, but when Harry describes something I have not seen, and a subject not often treated by poets, he is as effective. A good example is 'Trans-Siberian'. You don't need to have read Blaise Cendrars—the poem's subtitle says it is a "belated footnote" to him—to understand what it is like to travel on the Siberian railway, to smell its smells and to hear its sounds. No word in the English language is alien to his poetic vocabulary. Many contemporary poets might claim this is true for them, but often wrongly, because they are so "realistic" that they exclude more traditional subjects and words from their vocabulary. Harry never makes this mistake. Wordsworth's famous criticism of

Thomas Gray in his introduction to the *Lyrical Ballads* is relevant here. Harry's vocabulary includes both those sorts of words that Wordsworth criticises and those that he praises, and few modern poets can claim to do this. Anyone who doubts this has only to read the poem about Beethoven's late E Flat string quartet. This poem is, amongst other things, a beautiful verbal representation of the glories that result when a master composer at the height of his powers argues with the rules he imposes upon himself in the use of sonata form.

A lot of Harry's poetry is—I am sure unconsciously—didactic. It is not for nothing that he worked as a schoolteacher for many years, and he was an excellent one too: I was taught by him. It is typical of his tact that never once during his classes did he mention he wrote poetry or press any of his poetry upon us. Didacticism is often regarded as a fault in poetry, but I beg to differ, especially when the didacticism is incidental, but often interestingly incidental, to the poem's main theme. In the poem 'Joachim du Bellay, 1522–1560' you don't need to have read a word of du Bellay's poetry to pick up the melancholy and despair he felt during his exile in Rome. (One fact the poem does not convey, his early death, is cunningly supplied in the title). But the poem may lead a curious reader to discover more about Du Bellay, and if he is then impelled to find some of Du Bellay's poetry and read it, albeit in English, then something has been achieved beyond the immediate effect of the poem. An early poem of his, 'Matsushima (The Pine Islands)', is an excellent example of this. The poem has a complicated construction which is I am quite sure the reverse of accidental. One of the lines in the poem consists of one word only: "enisl'd". The word makes perfect sense in the context of the poem, and does not require the sort of note that T.S. Eliot was fond of in his poetry. But it contains, or rather is enfolded by, a clue: it is in inverted commas. A little research will tell you that the word is almost certainly a quotation from a poem by Matthew Arnold, and anyone who looks up this poem will find himself in a world parallel to, and reflecting, Harry's poem. Is Harry's poem incidentally a commentary on Arnold's? Perhaps: the truth is that a good poem can be many different things at the same time.

Although any good poem gains if it is read aloud, some need to be read to oneself first for the poem's construction and meaning to become clear. Many of Harry's poems fall into this category, and particularly 'Matsushima (The Pine Islands)' with its brackets and then brackets within brackets. Every single one of these poems gains from being read quietly to oneself. Only then do their subtle rhythms properly expose themselves. His syllabic verse particularly gains from such treatment. Reading aloud also exposes Harry's great technical skill. Many of his poems are unrhymed; but it is just as hard, if not harder, to write an unrhymed as a rhymed poem. Anyone who doubts his skill in rhyming has only to read the several sonnets scattered unobtrusively throughout his work. 'Barsoom', a description of the planet Mars in the John Carter novels of Edgar Rice Burroughs, is a good example of this. It is also another good example of the poet's ability to bring to life something unfamiliar to the reader; I know this because I have never read Burroughs' work. There are many other fine examples of Harry's technique in his translations, and here the book he has made from translating Victor Hugo's work comes immediately to mind. 'Boaz Asleep' is, unlike the original, *not* rhymed, but its rhythmical control is superb. You could step from this poem's world into that of Gray's famous ode and not notice any falling off in technique at all. This technique is an example of what Shelley somewhere calls "control", that is, the ability to have the exact poetical tool to hand to deal with any technical problem. You can be a great poet without possessing this—perhaps Blake is an example—but you emphatically cannot be a good poet without it. This technical mastery, very unusually, appears in Harry Guest's earliest published work. It would be interesting to know whether there is much unpublished immature work lurking in the background. I suspect too that Harry's own poetry gained from his translating. Are the 'English Poems' maybe that bit more English because of his immersion in Hugo's very French poetry? And is it over-fanciful to see in an entirely modern poem like 'A Daughter's First Term at University' the influence of Hugo's poems about his relationships with his children?

Victor Hugo was very much a Christian poet, somewhat of a rarity in 19th century France, and it is surely not a coincidence that Harry Guest chose to translate him, because Christianity, even more unusually in an English late 20th century poet, is fundamental to his work. In some poems this is obvious—the group of poems entitled 'fides', for example and in particular, 'Communion', and 'To David on his Ordination'—but in other cases, and indeed in most of his work, a Christian thread runs through his meaning and perhaps sometimes even exists without the poet himself realising it. Two poems chosen almost at random, 'The Artist at a Certain Age' and 'Impostor', make perfect sense when read entirely secularly, but gain in richness when we realise the poet is writing in a Christian context. In 'The Embassy of Heaven', when

> At nightfall the curtains
> Remain undrawn. Passers-by
> Catch a glimpse of mirrors,

we know that more than curtains and mirrors are being described, but what do they symbolise, and indeed are these words symbols at all? The reader must make up his own mind, and different readings may lead to different conclusions.

For some years Harry taught in Japan, at Yokohama University, and this long break from Britain had I think a profound and favourable effect on his poetry. Obviously his poems set in Japan are a new departure in his work, but more important I feel was his new feeling of Britishness reflected in his poetry on his return. I am going to look foolish if I am proved wrong, but I think the 'English Poems' published in the volume *Lost and Found* in 1983 were to some extent a reflection of his feelings on his return. I say "Britishness", despite having already called them English, because Welshness is another very important aspect of Harry's work. It is true that he has never lived in Wales as far as I know, but he was born there, is of Welsh descent and when he writes in 'Wales Re-Visited':

> At home I have had to live as an alien

I am sure he means every word. Later on in this poem he writes:

> A harper gives his message to the clouds.
> I do not understand the words he sings.
> I can no longer tell where I belong.

These are profoundly sad words, and there are many other similar expressions of melancholy in Harry's work. In 'Retrospective' he writes:

> Across the grass when I looked back
> My footprints made a temporary track,

Referring I think to his own work. So why is it that turning back to his work I feel a rush of anticipation for the fun I know I will get when I open that first page? Of course his firm Christian faith, not contradicted by the sadnesses in some poems, is one reason. Another is his intimate knowledge, often sadly unfashionable now in England, of the whole mainstream of European poetry from its beginnings (there are fine translations of Villon) right up to the present day, a knowledge which his translations and original poems richly show. Another is that control I mentioned before, an ability to stand back from his work, and indeed his whole poetic consciousness, and gaze at it with an effective similitude of calm.

None of these qualities leads to immediate popularity, but I do not think his work will be temporary. Time, as always, will have the last word. To misquote one of his own poems, I do not think that:

> Deep in the skull scraped free of images,
> The brutal regent will meet out the dark.

After all, regents rarely have the last word.

Peter France

A Translation for Harry

When Harry and I first met in the 1960s, we were both teachers of French. He was already a highly regarded poet, but he was also to become a great poet-translator. Not a maker of "versions", but a poet who worked from an intimate knowledge of the originals. He later described this work, laconically but suggestively, in a piece published in the yearbook *Comparative Criticism* (No. 14, 1992) and entitled "'Your Blood: Some Sort of Epic'; interpretation/translation of a poem by Alain Bosquet, "Ton Sang: Une Epopée'". Before that he had published his Penguin volume of *Post-War Japanese Poetry* (1972, translated with Lynn Guest and Kajima Shozo), and the volume that I particularly love, a selection of Victor Hugo, *The Distance, The Shadows* (Anvil, 1981).

Hugo has been translated into English of course, quite voluminously in the nineteenth century, but rarely very well. Perhaps some who might have made a good job of it were put off by his grandiose poetic rhetoric, the roll and thump of his rhyming alexandrines, often sustained over pages at a time. Harry must have had to teach Hugo often enough in school, and he had no doubt had to wrestle with André Gide's famous designation of France's greatest poet as "Victor Hugo, hélas!" But there is no such fastidious condescension in his own approach to Hugo, of whom he writes: "He is, finally, incomparable. If he can be classed within a French tradition at all it is that of Rabelais, Balzac and Proust himself, the tradition of daring all to come to terms with all. He has flaws as they have. But above all he is not afraid of the contradictions in life itself, not afraid of imperfections, nor of failure."

The preface to *The Distance, The Shadows* offers an admirable account of what the translator of poetry can aim at. Harry's essential aim is to translate Hugo's poems in such as way as to "share with other readers a poet I have admired all my adult life." His translations are therefore not what Dryden or Lowell might have called "imitations"; they are "as accurate as I can make them". This does not of course imply "word-for-word" translation (whatever that might be), and he baulks at the idea that his book could be used as a crib. His translations are "re-creations", with all that that implies in the reworking of word order and syntax. And above all, as he puts it, "Each poem has been translated on its own terms in an attempt to find a form appropriate to it in English". In some cases the form mirrors that of the original, elsewhere it seems like a new departure, but turns out to be what is needed to make the French poem live in English.

One such re-creation is 'The Rose in the Infanta's Hand' ('La Rose de l'Infante'), a haunting poem counterpointing a Velásquez-like image of an infanta in a rose garden by a pond with the images of armadas and sea battles in the mind of her watching father, Philip II. Here is a brief extract from a fairly long poem, evoking the vision of the king in sonorous alexandrines:

> C'est lui; l'homme en qui vit et tremble le royaume.
> Si quelqu'un pouvait voir dans l'œil de ce fantôme
> Debout en ce moment l'épaule contre un mur,
> Ce qu'on apercevrait dans cet abîme obscur,
> Ce n'est pas l'humble enfant, le jardin, l'eau moirée
> Reflétant le ciel d'or d'une claire soirée,
> Les bosquets, les oiseaux se bequetant entre eux,
> Non, au fond de cet œil comme l'onde vitreux,
> Sous ce fatal sourcil qui dérobe à la sonde
> Cette prunelle autant que l'océan profonde,
> Ce qu'on distinguerait, c'est, mirage mouvant,
> Tout un vol de vaisseaux en fuite dans le vent,
> Et dans l'écume, au pli des vagues, sous l'étoile,
> L'immense tremblement d'une flotte à la voile,
> Et là-bas, sous la brume, une île, un blanc rocher,
> Écoutant sur les flots ces tonnerres marcher.

Harry's version, with its generally short, unequal, unrhymed lines, might seem far removed from this, but it seems to me to convey, in a much lightened form, the complex poetic vision of the French text. Some things are much simplified, some expanded, and above all, the poem moves with an expressive rhythm—like Hugo's original, Harry's poem is made for the voice:

> The King: the man
> in whom the nation lives
> or trembles leans his shoulder on the wall.

In his dark gaze reflected is no child,
no garden, no stretch of water
shot with the colours of the evening,
no trees for the restive birds—instead,
across those eyes
as secret as the ocean pass
ships, a whole flight of ships, sails
billowing, sails
on the foam by starlight, sails
along the distance of the waves
and flickering in the dark.
Far off, an island in the mist
shows a white gleam of cliffs that echo
advancing thunder borne across the sea.

I can't match that, but in homage to a master-translator, let me none the less offer a translation of a Russian poem of homage to an Italian master. This is Osip Mandelstam's 'Ariosto', written in Stary Krym in May 1933, a time full of ominous developments in the poet's life, when he was seeking comfort in the example of an ancient Mediterranean culture. The last line, as readers of Russian folktales will recognize, is the formula by which the story teller rounds off his magical tale. Mandelstam too is incomparable:

Ariosto

The cleverest man in Italy, untroubled,
suave Ariosto feels a little hoarse.
He revels in his catalogue of fish,
peppers the oceans with malicious babble.

Like a musician playing on ten cymbals,
he tirelessly snaps off the thread of tales,
not knowing his own way, he pulls all ways
his mixed-up story of chivalric scandals.

On the cicadas' tongue, a captivating air—
Pushkinian sadness with southern conceit—
he catches Orlando in a web of lies
and shudders, feeling utterly transfixed.

And to the sea he says: Roar without thought.
And to the maiden on the rock: Lie bare…
Tell us more tales, then, we can't get enough,
as long as blood flows in us and ears hear…

O town of lizards, where there's not a soul!
If only you could give us more like him,
Dreary Ferrara… Hurry, yet again,
as long as blood flows in us, tell us tales…

It's cold in Europe, dark in Italy.
Power is repulsive, like a barber's hands.
But he still lords it better, cunningly,
and out through the wide open window sends

a smile to the hill lambs, and to the monk
on donkey-back, and to the ducal troops,
silly from wine and garlic and the plague,
and to the child that sleeps among blue flies.

But I love his unbridled freedom, love
his foolish language, sweetly salted tongue,
and the enchanting clash of double sounds—
I fear to cut the pearl from the bivalve.

Suave Ariosto, who knows, an age will pass—
and into a single wide fraternal blue
we'll pour your azure and our own black sea.
We too were there. And there we drank the mead.

Peter France

John Greening

To Sir Philip Sidney
cc Harry Guest

A few apologetic words about the art—and not just of poetry—
to you who were the paradigm of taste for your age. When you died,
what extremes of elegant grief. And we had Michael Jackson.

True, we did mark Shakespeare's birthday but it brought
the death of Peter Porter, too. A small cross
on most readers' ballot paper, and the gangs were out

skinning the Midlands. If yours was a golden age, ours
was aluminium at best, with a ring-pull, to be chucked
into the bushes. Or not that, even. The age of Lycra.

Skin-tight bikers free-wheeling out round Penshurst
who are art, perhaps, or poetry in motion, tale-spinners
or song-cyclists. The Porsche parked by Wilton House.

The hoarding of Stella's sparkle. Fly to Arcadia.
The Herbert franchise, Pembroke.com, these are art
because we've no idea what art is any more.

I'd like to say it has to offer beauty, but where
does that leave Bacon's screaming popes and bloody
carcasses (you'd know) or Harry Birtwistle tilting

at cooling towers from his labyrinth. It's the minotaur
in the living room, but you'd see where he's coming from,
how ugliness can glow: Satan, satire, elephant dung.

I'd like to think enlightenment, too. But there hangs Rothko
offering a glass of iced water. And another. Another.
Telling us nothing but the value of nothingness. And here's Ashbery

disconnecting everything from everything, while Banksy runs
painting holes in the nation's walls, then slips away
into a blue screening. Like you, we think it must break moulds

and unlike you we recognise the mould-breakers of your age,
your gloomy Dowland, your William Harvey stirred by the blood,
your good old Francis Bacon, still unsmoked, unhung,

but not for want of inquisition. Even our mould-makers
have gone, mouldering like their out-of-date puns.
We have no moulds. We want art to divert, though loopy

installations and minimal interest operas tell us
entertainment it ain't. If it wuz, then *Friends* and Dan Brown
would be art. *They are*, the echo comes from the Rosslyn Chapel

upriver from here. Is Sting? Are Guinness ads? Are the Sims
or the Simpsons? Clips? Apps? The i-God steps from its machine.
We have no standard, only plastic that can be swiped:

please wait while we authorise art, it says, welcome
to art, it says. And poetry is what those apes are playing with
in 2001. I could have used pentameter.

I could have gone HD, and strung you imagist prayer beads.
Instead, my claim to good art calls on something
our age worships, which Auden thought the litmus test

of bad art: sincerity. A species of it, anyhow,
whose origin lies in those 'many mysteries' you defended,
beneath my tapping fingers and my laptop like those caves

under Drummond's castle. Deserted caves. And not
in that deep well where people lean and gasp as poets
drop words in and vainly wait for some reply.

Hawthornden Castle

John Greening

A Review of *A Puzzling Harvest: Collected Poems 1955-2000* by Harry Guest

The time comes when every poet begins to wonder about a *Collected* edition. For some it never happens (where is Edmund Blunden's?), for some it happens again and again, each time radically revised or in a different format (Auden, and now even Larkin); for others, there is only a series of self-denying *Selected*s (Heaney, Dunn); while for a deceased élite there may even be a *Complete Poems*. It is a chronological record of achievement, a resource for fans and students, but a *Collected* also invites the newcomer to read through from beginning to end, like a biography. This is not always a rewarding experience, but in the case of Harry Guest, whose work has largely passed us by since the nineteen-sixties, it proves something of a revelation.

Guest has always been an enigma in contemporary English letters. Absent from most of the key reference books and landmark anthologies, he nevertheless featured in the original *Penguin Modern Poets* series and has been in Anvil Press' catalogue for four decades. Edward Lucie-Smith, who did include him in *British Poetry since 1945,* said he was "probably the nearest English equivalent to a West Coast American poet such as Gary Snyder" and Martin Booth's critical volume, *British Poetry 1964-84,* calls him "a stunning writer whose poetic vision relates all things into a unit". This new collection (flawlessly and accurately printed on good quality paper) is a chance to see that work as a unit. To those who know it at all, Guest's name will conjure something oriental, vaguely New Age, and, yes, Snyderish. There is a truth in this: he worked in Japan and has translated Japanese poetry. And there is an inescapably spiritual ambience to his work, an interest in pagan sites and and the rites of love. But it was not Snyder so much as A.R. Ammons that came to mind as I read *A Puzzling Harvest.* Guest's poetry is plain-spoken, limpid in its diction, but sinewy in its thought and the complexity of its forms, stanza, metre, line-patterning. The book is full of formal experiments, such as the filmic poems of the seventies (including a mini-screenplay 'The Inheritance') and the longer lines of his superb 'Elegies' from the eighties. He is neither a witty nor a lyrical poet, and there is little overt musicality (not much internal rhyme or other sound effects); only a tribute to Vernon Watkins reminds us that he was born in Wales yet chose to shun the school of Welsh hyperbole. Just as only the odd reference to Beethoven's late quartets or Paul Klee reminds us that he is a learned man. He wears his bardic mantle lightly, staying as far as possible from 'performance poetry' yet retaining clarity, honesty and accessibility.

Guest's early work is, however, discouraging: little more than an index of first loins:

> To rape the air, the dark air of night,
> burying an ice-like orgasm in clouds—
> thrown backwards on the globe, splayed there,
> moist legs apart and her frail perfume
> lingering in the nostril. Sunrise.

This is the least interesting side of Guest, but it feeds the later, less heated work, and even at this stage there is a more subtle Cavafy-like mode in some of his narratives and sketches (the blank verse 'Portrait from Memory', for example) with their mildly ironic note and their civilized cadences. And sudden gems catch the eye: 'A Creed for Our Time' suggests the riches to come, as do one or two that show the beginnings of his fascination with landscape and wider cultural issues. Generally, however, patience is required reading the first hundred or so pages: the sequences are too abstract and long-drawn-out, too self-obsessed (although, paradoxically, 'Autobiography' is objective and compelling), carrying too much of the nineteen-sixties with them.

As Guest begins to move beyond himself, writing about the experience of fatherhood in 'An Autumn Record', or other cultures (the Buddhist Festival of the Dead) in 'Two Poems for O-Bon', the poetry draws formal and emotional strength:

> Clean the altars.
>   Scour
> the wood remembering
> dead next of kin.
>   Their ashes
> are gathering energy, emit to love
> remembered presences.

> Let
> the temple-bell vibrate.
>
> Clean the altars.
>   Prepare
> the past, a welcome for the past.
>
> And, waiting, pray.

Japanese culture fascinates him, perhaps because of its sensitivity to nature, perhaps because of its preoccupation with death, the sensuality of the attendant rites, the awareness of "phantoms/hiding behind peonies". His interest in the exotic is developed in his 1970 collection *The Cutting Room*, which is full of impressionistic detail of his travels. The journey is a recurrent metaphor, whether it be the powerful 'Half-way Query', which begins: "The sudden tunnel: my reflection/in pale, translucent colours rides the wall" or his contemplation of how the needle travels a record groove as he and his wife listen to Schumann—"the madness waiting/at the long end of/a black-cut spiral"—in the extended syllabics of 'Anniversary'. Like A.R. Ammons, he weaves social commentary with diary entry, abstract analysis with close observation. He questions as he quests—and love is always the implied answer, but love's spiritual potential is tapped more and more as Guest approaches middle age.

'Miniatures' was composed when ill health obliged his wife and son to remain behind while he and his daughter visited Oshima in 1971. Like Ted Hughes' 'Pike' and Coleridge's 'Lime-tree Bower' (even the work of Noh poet Zeami, whose creative exile Guest writes about elsewhere) this sequence is a testament to the fecundity of deprivation. The delicacy here is remarkable, his use of the broken form, with its suggestive spaces. It is the first really moving sequence in the book, the first that made me want to slow down and re-read. This is the ninth of thirty-six short poems:

> She laughs her way up the dunes
> as dark as negatives
>   Looks round
> light-footed
> encouraging her slipping

> father
>   Notes though like me
> no symmetry
> two absences

'Miniatures' uses a genuinely free, imagistic verse to explore Guest's feelings not only towards his family, but about the environment, human responsibility and identity, the transience of contemporary culture, the inevitability of decay. Again, his openness to new form pays dividends: there is a sense of psychological drama, the silences pointing up key words. The sequence becomes very abstract, but because we know the context, we are reassured:

> Leaves whirl wherever
> and the colours fall
>   To catch
> in middle age
> the relish of impermanence
> and feel
> belonging to a world of shift
>   The children
> losing a charm to gain one daily
> blending if they're allowed
> into a transience

'Miniatures' marks a change. As Guest writes in 'Lovers' (from his 1983 collection, 'Lost and Found'): "There is no thread that leads past blind/alleys of lust on down/the corridors of remembrance/to where the lovers stand/trapped in the labyrinth of time." He accepts the new world facing him and the poet that grows from his approaching middle age is all the better for it. He now sees his place in time, with a geological perspective, as in 'Landscape, South Dorset', which echoes Hardy's 'At Castle Boterel'. The landscape of the West Country (he lives in Exeter) enriches these later poems and offsets the sparse Japanese vision of earlier pages. But above all it is the deepening and ever more accessible religious instinct that strikes the reader, beginning with 'Communion' and moving through to 'The Cleansing', a narrative of Christ turning out the money-changers. This is not to say that these poems are narrowly Christian: there is a pagan impulse in Guest's love of standing stones, burial mounds, hill-forts, which feature increasingly. In forging a new relationship with the past through landscape, he also discovers a new sense of Englishness (see his sequence of 'English poems'). But the love of ritual (more use of repetition, for instance), the self-scrutiny ('Death of a Friendship'), the attention to questions of an after-life—these seem to grow out of this new religious feeling. His 'Elegies' are among the most striking poems of his middle years. Often provocatively prosaic, mixing tenses and registers, they are long-lined meditations on time, the nature of reality, poetry and the supernatural. Guest finds momentum in dream-like free-association, taking us to the edge of reason, but also (particularly in his consciousness of words' inadequacy) harking back to 'Four Quartets': "Unseen, always,/the wonder of speckled egg, of shrivelled leaf/and the seed-case is matched by the wonder/of fossil and rainbow. This is "the interchange/of faith and belief".

Subsequent work includes further experiment, responses to music and art, to travel and history, but above all to landscape. There are inevitably more occasional poems, and naturally there is the older writer's growing sense of frustration and loss ("Paths under town and tarmac/lead no longer to the sacred places") but he is essentially an optimist: in 'Memories of the Sinagua'—one of several late poems where he finds a consistent, unadorned and authoritative narrative voice—he describes a volcanic eruption in Arizona which displaced the native people, but then made their lands more fertile so they could return. And he is always ready to see his own life in the context of the wider picture, to trace his life's highlights in the rings of a tree-stump, then to remember: "they only recorded/the history of the wind". What finally brings home the wider significance of *A Puzzling Harvest* is the selection of translations that crown the book: Ronsard, Nerval, Rilke, Brecht, Serafini *et al*, followed by twenty-five haiku from the Japanese. It is time for a reassessment of this first-rate poet.

John Hall

A Sonnet of Sorts, for Harry

Harry Guest eighty years in
An age of lyricism can[not] be said to have ended
Remembering frankly loves friendships lusts
Reality / sometimes occurs in a poem you said and
You can train the intellect you said too but

Gleefully baffled blessed the lesson in kissing
Unimportant aspects of the day last in your syllabic attention
Each dawn each line renewing a quite specific loss
Summoning an allegory perhaps tied always to the literal
The fact that they're here now your poems proves to be

A portrait you did of yourself
The room holds the bright harvest whose light puzzles you

8 lines and another judicious volta, another jolt of memory
0 Harry the way you listen to those distant lusts and loves

Many of the constituent parts of this poem are stolen and adapted, without the poet's permission, from *A Puzzling Harvest* and *Some Times*. This little piece inevitably fails to register the astonishing and sustained quality and generosity of Harry's work, the way he was able to tune a poem so that it could deal with almost anything that he did, saw, read, heard, felt, remembered; and that he has never let up the attentiveness of his ear and its connections to lungs, mouth and heart—this last both literal and, yes indeed, metaphoric.

Christopher Hampton

Harry Guest, translator

> I who heard in trembling across a waste of leagues
> The turgent stroms and Behemoths moan their rut,
> I weaving for ever voids of spellbound blue,
> Now remember Europe and her ancient ramparts.

Alternatively,
> I who flinched hearing fifty leagues away
> Behemoths rutting where the Maelstrom swirls—
> Lone threader of the blue immobile day—
> I now miss Europe with her time-worn walls!

Or, as Rimbaud put it:
> Moi qui tremblais, sentant geindre à cinquante lieues
> Le rut des Béhémots et des Maelstroms épais,
> Fileur éternel des immobilités bleues,
> Je regrette l'Europe aux anciens parapets.

The first extract is from Samuel Beckett's translation of Rimbaud's masterpiece 'Bateau Ivre' ('Drunken Boat', Beckett called it, accurately enough); the second is from Harry Guest's translation of the same stanza in the poem (which he calls, rather more imaginatively, 'Craft Half Seas Over'). As can be seen, Beckett, who made the translation in the early thirties for 700 francs, which he used to relocate from Paris to London, favours rough, unrhyming Alexandrines and the kind of ostentatiously recondite vocabulary ("turgent stroms") that often tempted the adolescent Rimbaud himself. Harry, on the other hand, writing fifty years or more later, risks the slight constriction of the iambic pentameter (as natural though to English as the Alexandrine is to French) and shoulders the burden of rhymes and half-rhymes. Yet consider how much more graceful, simple and evocative his version is. "Flinched", to begin with, conveys the feeling of "tremblais" far more accurately than "trembled"; "fifty leagues" is more correctly specific; "fileur" perhaps relates to "filer" (to slip away or cut and run) in a way analogous to "thread" and "tread"; and the famous "anciens parapets" (which I rendered in my play about Rimbaud, inspired by and dedicated to Harry, as "the dusty mantelpiece of Europe") is beautifully caught by "time-worn walls", which the poet indeed misses, rather than just remembers.

None of this is intended in any way to disparage Beckett, whom Harry has always worshipped this side of idolatry, as can be seen in his 1961 poem about Beckett, written only a few years after *Godot*, while Beckett's immense reputation was still in the making. Indeed, I remember my own introduction to Beckett, a broadcast of *Endgame* (no doubt with Patrick Magee and Jack MacGowran) via Harry's substantial wireless; and my reaction, a mixture of bafflement and fascination, stimulated by Harry's infectious enthusiasm. On the contrary, my purpose here is to suggest that even Beckett, who came into his own as a remarkable translator of himself, cannot begin to match, in this instance, the grace and inventiveness of Harry's translation.

Translation is a particular hobby-horse of mine. I have practised it myself throughout my career in the theatre, one of the few mediums in which translators are adequately rewarded. Most translation is charity work. My first professional translating job was to rework an existing translation, made only for publication, of Isaac Babel's play, *Marya*, by two distinguished translators, Michael Glenny and Harold Shukman. The translation's curious inconsistency of tone was explained by the fact that the translators had worked, alone, on alternate scenes. "Well, you know," one of them said to me, "in translation, you get paid by the yard." Put another way, in order to make a living as a translator in prose or poetry, you have to work at inordinate speed and resign yourself to obscurity, neglect and every shade of under-estimation. And the downgrading of language teaching, the complacent insularity of the English-speaking world, the sheer self-righteousness of ignorance, all conspire towards a general deterioration of the conditions of the trade.

And yet translators are invaluable; the importance of their work can scarcely be overstated.

Harry is an inspiring teacher; in my case, he was responsible for igniting a love of French and German writing, especially of the 19th and early 20th centuries, which has been the backbone of my working life. It was he who persuaded me, when I was planning to slope off to university and read English, like everybody else, to opt for French and German instead and thus gain privileged access to two other literatures.

And to make Baudelaire and Rimbaud, Flaubert and Stendhal, Goethe and Rilke come alive so vividly and with so contemporary a spirit to adolescent schoolboys: what else is that but a form of profoundly valuable translation? To be an intermediary, a key with the power to open young imaginations: is that not the translator's ideal?

In conclusion, here's the second half of Harry's translation of Baudelaire's exquisitely melancholy 'Recueillement':

> Come, sorrow, now, give me your hand – they've gone
>
> Away—we'll watch the dead years in their creased
> Outdated dresses lean on heaven's rail,
> Regret rise smiling from the river-bed,
>
> Beneath an arch the dying sunlight fail,
> And, like a long shroud dragging in the east,
> Hear, dear one, hear night's soft approaching tread.

As Baudelaire is to Poe, the interpreter of a sensibility, an intensely sympathetic travelling companion and selfless impresario, so Harry is to Baudelaire.

Christopher Hampton

David Hare

In 1960, I was thirteen years old. I'd certainly never met a poet and I didn't expect to. Lancing College, a High Anglican school with a massively imposing chapel on the South Downs, had barely recovered from the war. It was full of elderly masters in grey turn-up flannels, and herringbone jackets with leather patches. When Harry Guest turned up to teach modern languages, relatively fresh from university, he stood out startlingly in a school culture which seemed to have been formed half by Benjamin Britten and half by Stanley Matthews. In drainpipe trousers, and chic button-down shirts and slim knitted ties, Harry didn't look like his colleagues—his loping walk was inimitable, though not for want of boys trying—and with his eloquent enthusiasm for all things continental, he most certainly didn't sound like them either.

Harry was not only my first poet, he was also my first intellectual. The names coming from his lips—Rimbaud, Baudelaire, Sartre—were not at that time common currency in West Sussex. Harry introduced me to a life of ideas. At the end of each term, I would ask him for a reading list, which he would set down in his immaculate handwriting. Back at home, I would work my way doggedly through Forster, Balzac, Koestler, Wells, Camus and Ford Madox Ford, without necessarily understanding much of what I was reading, but knowing that, come the new term, Harry would want to know what I thought of them. When, at the end of my time at Lancing, Cyril Connolly published a list of the 100 Greatest Books of the Century in the *Sunday Times*, I had read 62. Entirely thanks to Harry.

I never felt he was as keen on me as I was on him, but I can't say it ever bothered me. You can't have everything. A few years ago, I read his book on artists' view of artists, and it was clear at once that because I had worked in the collaborative rather than the solitary arts, my idea of literature's purpose had necessarily been much more rough-and-tumble than his own. If the word were not so stupid with misuse, you could call Harry an aesthete. But the disagreements you have with a great teacher are just as formative as the things you discover in common.

It's possible I was drawn to him as much for his enviable life-style as for his values. At weekends he would go to London, and if we were lucky in Monday's French class, we would get told stories about the parties he had been to. We had deduced from his suitably slim first volume of poems that "Mike and Joan who don't take me seriously" must be Michael and Joan Bakewell. And sure enough, they had both been present when, late one Saturday night in a darkened room, the young dramatist Harold Pinter had swung a punch at a man who had made an anti-Semitic remark. This gave me an exotic idea of London's bohemian night life to which it has rarely since lived up.

Giving the inaugural Evelyn Waugh lecture at Lancing College in 2008, I described a particular night in his flat over a shop in Shoreham when Harry gave a dinner party for some pupils with his then-fiancée Lynn. At a certain point in the evening, after the main course, I think, but before the pudding, he produced a copy of George Steiner's much admired book *The Death of Tragedy*, which was ominously covered in black scrawls, and remarked that nobody could be expected to take seriously a work which confused the Duke of Gloucester with King Lear. Everyone *knew*, he said, with terrifying emphasis, everyone *knew* that it was the blinded Gloucester who tried to throw himself off a beach, thinking it a cliff. But Steiner carelessly had it down as being Lear. In disgust, Harry then threw the book into a waste-paper basket and burst into tears.

As I observed in the lecture, it was certainly one of the most unforgettable moments of my young life. In a repressed post-war childhood, I had often seen adults' passions erupt unexpectedly in unexpected places, but never had I seen anyone driven to such lengths by a mere book. The lesson I learned that night, for good or ill, was that there were people who thought literature enormously important, as important, it seemed, as life or love. Since then I have witnessed a good few pieces of violent behaviour brought on by real or imaginary deficiencies in works of art, but I have never seen a reaction so pure and purely devoid of self-consciousness. Harry could not endure a work he thought bad.

If I was bored when I finally went to university, it was largely because I had already enjoyed university teaching of the highest standard, both from Harry and from his more conservative colleague Donald Bancroft. School-teaching, I had been told, was about drilling and instruction, whereas university teaching would be about example and inspiration. In my life, at least, it was the other way round. School was charged with the unexpected: Flaubert one day, Vernon Scannell the next, each one lovingly explained and set in context. All this I owe to Harry. I've not seen or heard from him from that day to this.

Lee Harwood

Harry Guest – "Splendid!"

In October 1963 a group of poets and a be-bop band went down in a van to Lancing College near Shoreham-by-sea in Sussex. We were there to present an evening of jazz and poetry marking the launch of *Night Scene* magazine. It was here that I first met Harry Guest. He was then teaching French and German at the college. I don't remember too much of that evening except that the students were very enthusiastic and some of the staff were not so enthusiastic. The school chaplain walked out in disgust, later calling the event "an ignoble experience". This, of course, immensely pleased us, young "rebels" of the early 1960s.

But the important thing for me now is that I met Harry and started a friendship that has lasted almost 50 years. A friendship that has always been so rich because of Harry's natural enthusiasm, generosity and his wide knowledge of so many subjects. Learning from each other's enthusiasms is one of the greatest boosts I know to becoming a writer. Our shared enthusiasms ranged from poetry and literature, of course, to history and especially prehistory, painting, music, films, Wales, and, maybe most of all, the countryside, walking and clambering around in the hills and mountains and plodding across the moors.

Over the years we have often lived far apart so letters have been our main form of contact. I note that I have in an old shoebox a collection of over 360 letters from Harry. As well as these I have the vivid memories of our meetings and, when we could arrange them, our expeditions.

How do you measure out such a friendship? There are photos and notebooks, but most of all, just like flash cards, memories and pictures come into my head, often when least expected.

I remember visiting Harry in Brighton in the 1960s. After a testing mulligatawny soup and a curry at an Indian restaurant near the Palace Pier we'd drive along the coast road to Shoreham in Harry's car, a low-slung black car with running boards. It should have been a Citroën in a French detective film, but I've since learnt it was a ten-horse-power MG saloon. There was much talk of Cocteau.

After Harry's six years stay in Japan, where he and his wife Lynn had university teaching jobs, he settled in Exeter. This gave us

12th October. 1963. at Lancing College, Lancing, Sussex.

NIGHT SCENE
an evening of poetry and jazz

8:00	jazz by the Inigo Kilborn Quintet
8:30	Neil Oram, Ginge Grierson, Peter Jay read
9:00	Peter Jay reads Catullus' "Attis" with the Inigo Kilborn Quintet
9:10	Interval with jazz
9:20	Lee Harwood, Harry Guest, Peter Jay, Bal Parr read
9:45	Lee Harwood reads an extract from his translation of Tristan Tzara's "the almost perfect man" with the I.K.Q.
9:50	jazz by the Inigo Kilborn Quintet

* * *

The idea for this reading sprang out of the publication of Lee Harwood's book "NIGHT SCENE", which is a collection of poems by (mainly) Londoners, & has as its common theme urban life. The poets are not a defined group, politically or even poetically: the complexity of urban life makes this impossible. All they do have in common is their avant-garde poetic outlook and a lack of public recognition. The gulf between poet & audience is great; this reading is an attempt to bridge that gap.
P.A.C.J.

* * *

jazzmen: <u>Inigo Kilborn</u> (trumpet), ex-student of Queen Mary College, London. At present schoolteaching with a view to leaving that profession for a musical career.

<u>Len Brown</u> (piano), on a post-graduate research course at Queen Mary College.

<u>Hugh Lang</u> (tenor sax), in pharmaceutical development.

<u>Joe Kirby</u> (bass), currently at the Royal College of Music.

<u>Lance Ganney</u> (drums), a nomad clerk.

poets: Lee Harwood, b. 1939, B.A. English, lives in Stepney, edits NIGHT SCENE, published in 'Poetmeat', 'O Leo'.

Ginge Grierson, the Don Quixote of West London, works in a Youth Employment Office, published in 'Poetmeat'.

Harry Guest, b. 1932, Wales, educated Cambridge, Sorbonne, published in 'delta', 'Outposts', 'The Poetry Review'; 'Private View' published 1962, at present working on a novel.

Peter Jay, b. 1945, O.L., going up to Oxford this term, published in 'Poetmeat', 'Breakthru', translations of Catullus 'I hate and love' published 1963.

Neil Oram, b. 1938, at present a gardener in London. Painter and unpublished poet. Travels include Rhodesia, Turkey, Syria, Jordan. Plans to go to Tangier.

Bal Parr, gardener's labourer in Dagenham. Poems in 'O Leo', 'Poetmeat'.

C. Valerius Catullus, b. 84B.C. Verona, lived in Rome where he became her first important avant-garde poet. Died at age of 30, unhappily in love.

Tristan Tzara, b. 1896 Roumania, founded 'Dada' 1916 in Zurich. 'L'homme approximatif' 1936 perhaps his most important work. His manifesto on art appeared in 1933 'Antitête'. At present living in Paris.

the opportunity for long walks across Dartmoor visiting the many prehistoric sites he was discovering. Sites such as the Merrivale and Stalldown stone rows and, best of all, The Grey Wethers stone circles. His favourite picnic on these expeditions was hard boiled eggs and a pork pie, something I've as yet to acquire a taste for. It always seemed to be summer.

From the 1970s onwards we started hill-walking and mountain-scrambling in North Wales. Spurred on by W. A. Poucher's guide *The Welsh Peaks*—Poucher's "day job" was as chief parfumier for Yardleys—we attempted a whole series of "interesting" routes. Some times the results were magical, other times somewhat demanding. Seeing a Brocken Spectre one January day on the snow-covered summit of Carnedd Llewellyn. Crouching beneath a rock face in a hail-storm halfway up Tryfan when the impact of the horizontal hail made the guidebook's text run into black smudges. "There is always another day," some descending climbers wisely advised us.

We later started visiting South Wales with marvellous crisp clear days on the Brecon Beacons. And once, further west, on the Black Mountain in the Carmarthen Fan where we were caught in a "white out" Harry almost stepped from the snow cloaked ridge into space, but luckily didn't. The mountain gods smiled on us again.

Such trips filled one with such a hunger that one just wanted more. Even driving back to Exeter we'd stop and go up and down the Sugar Loaf near Abergavenny as a last minute extra.

By the end of the 1990s there weren't as many mountain expeditions. Instead we would tour Cornwall visiting the prehistoric sites such as Zennor Quoit and Chun Quoit or go for gentler walks around Killerton near Exeter or along the banks of the Teign. The limitations of what doctors—smiling and nodding their heads—call the "ageing process" were gradually felt. The scale of the expeditions was reduced from earlier marathons. But as the saying goes "never mind the width, feel the cloth".

I remember Ric Caddel telling me of his taking Harry to visit Durham Cathedral. At a spiral staircase that went up to the cathedral's roof Harry shot ahead. All Ric could hear were exclamations of "splendid!" "marvellous!" from above. This memory has always seemed a perfect example of Harry's virtues. His enthusiasm and energy. Qualities I've admired from the start.

I'll leave it to others more capable than I to talk of Harry as a poet, prose writer and translator. All I can say is that I will always owe him a great debt as a poet. He showed me a precision and subtlety in his poems that I've always greatly valued and drawn on, and will continue to do so.

Happy Birthday Harry! May the day, the whole year, be filled with many pleasures great and small.

Jeremy Hilton

Meadow pipits, younger legs
(a mountain triptych for Harry Guest at 80)

   1

turning back shortly before the summit
of Grisedale Pike, I mourn

my younger legs, I grieve
a possible loss of mountaintops

and envy the meadow pipits
their freedom on the wind

the bird-books say their flight is weak
but that is a merely human view

no bird that inhabits
for 7 months a year
windswept mountain slopes
and survives in great numbers
cuckoos' nest invasions
egg-thieving ravens
mugging by merlins
can be truly considered weak in flight

and look, there is a merlin
floating across the path in front of me
on its slender curved wings
and the pipits have all gone
hidden in heather and rough grass
gone to ground by sudden instinct

I'm glad I turned back when I did
and will return to the mountains
the merlin, the meadow pipits

2

Harry, the birds of Spring
        are about to return
and the world like the flooding sea
    will wash
across our wintry shores
calling the streams falling from higher fells
streams with their rocks and dippers
tumbling icy over rapids
perhaps we are like those streams now
                you and me
journeying through our lives
with the tang of the mountaintop
        in our souls
but always descending
        towards a slower passage
                across flatlands

3

a smudge of mist
        hiding the ridge
ravens rasp from somewhere
        within the cloud or closer
a glimpse of the glide
        black, sailing with the wind
lashing wind I lean into
hoping these creaky legs
        can keep me upright
last mountain I climbed
        maybe the very last
if those legs will no longer
        will me the long uphill

so let's hope, Harry, for
reclaiming our younger legs
and many more mountains
        for us both

Andrew Houwen

'These islands   gathering images':
the Guests in Japan

Harry Guest's arrival in Japan on 16 September 1966 to take up a teaching post at Yokohama National University was the result of an accident. Guest had been expecting a move to Nigeria, not Japan, after his interview with the British Council. On reading in the newspapers about a beheaded corpse found on a Lagos golf course, however, Guest and his wife, Lynn, decided against Nigeria. The report would have been one of countless horror stories from Nigeria after the 1966 military coup and the ensuing civil war. Even before the coup, Nigeria was a dangerous place for British academics: in 1965, three British professors at Lagos University had been told to pack their bags after the vice-chancellor had been stabbed by students demonstrating against his appointment. The university suspended almost all its students and remained closed for months.[1]

If the Guests had thought they could avoid such situations by their move to a newly prosperous, peaceful Japan, they were mistaken. From 1967, several Japanese universities were shut down for months as a result of student demonstrations.[2] Yokohama National University was no exception. Guest recalls being pelted with stones by students when going in to collect his salary, which was still being paid even after the university had been shut down. Because of this, the university's bursar had to arrange to meet Guest in a furtive bar to hand over his wages. Guest offered lessons at his home, but eventually the university decided that the Guests were free to return to the UK. It was during their brief return that the Guests first met the poet and translator Nikos Stangos, who would collaborate with Guest on *Penguin Modern Poets 16* (1970) and *Post-War Japanese Poetry* (1972).

Guest also formed fruitful relationships with Japanese poets. In 1967, he first met Seiichi Niikuni, a Japanese concrete poet who lived two underground stops away from the Guests. Guest and Niikuni

---

[1] 'Vice-Chancellor Stabbed in Lagos', *The Times*, 09/06/1965, p. 10; 'Suspension of 600 Students', *The Times*, 11/06/1965, p. 12.
[2] Fred Emery, 'Japan Bewildered by Wave of Student Rebellion', *The Times*, 12/04/1967, p. 10.

first met when Angus Wilson wanted to meet some Japanese concrete poets; Guest arranged for Wilson to meet Niikuni. Guest and Niikuni became friends and spent many hours together at Niikuni's house experimenting with multilingual sound collages on cassettes. Some of these were performed at a concrete poetry festival.[3] Although no trace of their cassette experiments remains, their friendship resulted in the publication of three of Guest's concrete poems and an article ('Heritage and Peril') on concrete poetry by Guest in *ASA* (*Association of the Study of the Arts*), edited by Niikuni; and six of Niikuni's concrete poems were published in the Guests' anthology, *Post-War Japanese Poetry*.[4] His three concrete poems include a representation of a Henry Moore sculpture out of the words 'Henry Moore'; 'Vocabulary', which includes French, German, and English words scattered across the page; and 'Kanji Game'. The latter was the result not only of Guest's contact with Niikuni but also of his fascination with the Japanese language. 'Kanji Game' shows how ideograms are, in a sense, proto-concrete poems. As Guest writes in 'Heritage and Peril', "Concrete poetry plays with the relationship between various components. Once you've grasped the meaning plus the pure sound of each individual component you are able to put them together to see a different whole". For "Concrete poetry" one could substitute "*kanji*", as 'Kanji Game' demonstrates:

```
t       WHITE
 h
  r     wa
   e
  a     ter
 d
```

Six other *kanji* are included in the poem, but this one most aptly suggests its own composition by the threading/reading together of its components to form 'a different whole'. As the key included with the concrete poem explains, this cluster represents the formation of the *kanji* for 'track', 線 (*sen*). The top right part is indeed 'white' (白) and the bottom right is water (水); but the concrete poem does

---

[3] 'Niikuni Seiichi and I have been working on a couple of "sound-collages" in Japanese and English which are to have their (taped) first renderings next week at a concrete poetry fest', Guest, letter to Stangos, 02/06/1970.

[4] Guest, 'Henry Moore', 'Kanji Game', 'Vocabulary', *ASA*, no. 5 (1971), p. 18, p. 40, p. 41; Guest, 'Heritage and Peril', *ASA*, no. 4 (1970), pp. 8-10.

not accurately give the etymology of the *kanji*: the right hand side, 泉 (*sen*, 'spring'), is in fact a sound component of the character and the left hand side, 糸 ('thread') is the semantic component. Guest was doubtless aware of this but knew, also, that the composition of *kanji* offers a range of imaginative possibilities if the sound components are read semantically. With just these three words, a beautiful image is rendered both by the meaning of the words and by the page layout. To what extent this approach, similar to Pound's "ideogrammic method", affects Guest's poetry merits further investigation. In any case, 'Kanji Game' shows how he was keen to interact with Japanese poets and learn Japanese.

Niikuni was by no means the only Japanese poet with whom Guest interacted. In 1968, William Elliott and Kazuo Kawamura founded the Kanto Poetry Center at Kantō Gakuin University. It became a meeting place for Western and Japanese poets and was attended by, among others, Gary Snyder, James Kirkup, Shuntarō Tanikawa, and Guest himself. It was through the Center that he met many of the poets included in *Post-War Japanese Poetry*. Foremost among these were Toyoichirō Miyoshi, Yasuo Fujitomi and Tarō Kitamura. All three were considered important poets in Japan; their poetry was published in the *Shichōsha* series of contemporary poets in 1970, 1973, and 1975 respectively—roughly equivalent to being published by Faber & Faber. Considering that Guest had not read any modern Japanese poetry before his departure to Japan, the selection for his anthology was remarkably up to date with Japan's poetry scene. This was partly helped by Miyoshi's generosity in offering his library of contemporary Japanese poetry and his advice. As Guest wrote to Stangos, Miyoshi "lent us dozens of out-of-print books and was always willing to ring up any poet whose work had ambiguities or opacities".[5] These books, according to Guest, consisted even of poets that Miyoshi did not like but nevertheless thought would be representative of a particular strand of contemporary Japanese poetry. This is reflected in the diversity of poems selected in *Post-War Japanese Poetry*: alongside Niikuni's concrete poems, formally experimental poems such as those of Yasuo Irisawa mix with the more restrained, lyrical poetry of Kitamura. The Guests' ability to network effectively in the Japanese poetry world resulted in an accurate and representative anthology of post-war Japanese poetry.

Miyoshi had been introduced to the Guests by Shōzō Kajima, a poet, painter, and translator of William Faulkner who, like Guest,

---

[5] Guest, letter to Stangos, 03/06/1971.

taught at Yokohama National University. The Guests collaborated with him on *Post-War Japanese Poetry*. He wrote draft translations, after which the Guests would make them 'into reasonable English poems'.[6] But the Guests' desire for fidelity to the originals is shown in Guest's letter to Stangos: "he [Kajima] is very important [...] it is vital that in my tinkering none of the original nuances are lost—i.e. I shall re-cast the poems and test the versions out with him in scrupulous detail".[7] They are not only faithful to the nuances of meaning but also to what the Guests describe in their introduction as "the actual architecture of the original, the mere look of the lines, the assonances, verbal cross-references or contrasts".[8] This fidelity is especially evident in Tarō Naka's 'Fautrier's Birds' and Irisawa's 'Shining'.[9] Naka's original poem is strongly alliterative, suggesting the smooth sweeps of a late Fautrier abstract. The translation responds to this with a similar sweep of assonantal and alliterative patterns. It opens:

> Fautrier's picture of four birds
> One purple
> One green
>   The two remaining ones,
> transparent,
> skim through space in a magnetic storm
> scud through the gouache as
>   amazing amethyst
>   troubled emerald
>   Sharply [...]

The sibilance of transparent/skim/space/storm/scud reflects the original's alliteration in *kūkan no kasume*, "skim through space"; the translation replicates the original's alliteration (muradatsu murasaki / midareru midori) with its own ("amazing amethyst") or consonantal echoing ("troubled emerald"); and the shape of the translated poem on the page is also responsive to the original, with "Sharply" isolated as it is in the original.[10] In a letter to Stangos, Guest emphasises his intention to carry across the formal characteristics of Naka's original:

---

[6] Guest, letter to Stangos, 11/12/1970.
[7] Ibid.
[8] *Post-War Japanese Poetry*, p. 27.
[9] Ibid., pp. 88-9, p. 130.
[10] Tarō Naka, *Naka Tarō Shishū* (Tokyo: Shichōsha, 1968), pp. 61-2.

Climbing world
Hurled time

This was an attempt to catch the assonance of the original:
Senkai suru sekai
Jiten suru jikan[11]

The attempt was successful: again, the translation balances the preservation of a large part of the meaning with that of the original's assonance in the echoing of "cl*i*mbing / t*i*me" and "*w*orld / h*u*rled". Poetry is music, like the "orchestral arrangement" of Mallarmé, the subject of Guest's MA dissertation at the Sorbonne; but poetry is also a picture, as Guest's poems and indeed Mallarmé's 'Un Coup de dés' show. Irisawa's poem '*Kirakira Hikaru*' ('Shining') is translated in italics to render the original's *katakana*, one of the three Japanese scripts used for emphasis or for foreign words. In the original, the poem is formed of a rectangular block of 14 lines with 15 syllables each.[12] The phrase *kirakira hikaru* (キラキラヒカル) moves diagonally across the poem from bottom right to top left, with the suggestion that the fifteenth line would be a return to the first line. I have highlighted the diagonal movement of *kirakira hikaru* in bold type:

テツカヲナンオルカヒラキラキ
キタエモヲナツオルカヒラキラ
ラキルツモトリナオルカヒラキ
キラキテツフノベンオルカヒラ
ラキラキテタオノナナサルカヒ
ヒラキラキリカサガベカオルカ
カヒラキラキネカモニナンサル
ルカヒラキラキナツイヲナカサ
オルカヒラキラキタレカモナイ
ンナルカヒラキラキタツカヲフ
ナミホルカヒラキラキテツカヲ
ハダシヨルカヒラキラキタツダ
ナヲダミオルカヒラキラキタシ
イダラチカサルカヒラキラキテ
タシダヲネカオルカヒラキラキ

---

[11] Guest, letter to Stangos, 06/07/1971.
[12] Yasuo Irisawa, *Irisawa Yasuo Shishū* (Tokyo: Shichōsha, 1970), pp. 13-14.

The translation not only reflects the content of the original with remarkable accuracy; it also responds to the original's shape on the page. The title runs vertically downwards, with the rest of the poem intersecting this column diagonally from top left to bottom right:

> taking out my shining wallet i
>   bought a shining fish & also
>   a shining girl having bought the
>   shining fish i put it into a
>   shining
> pan held by the still shining
> girl then with the shining fish
>   also the shining change back under
>   those shining stars when suddenly
>   shining
> tears now dropping shining from
>   her eyes the shining girl wept

Guest's sense of responsibility towards the form of the original is rooted in his understanding, expressed in 'Heritage and Peril' and demonstrated in 'Kanji Game', of the poem as a picture. This sensitivity to the multiple signifying aspects of a poem—not just to the meaning of its words, but to its sounds and its shape on the page—and the ability to bring these aspects into the translations makes *Post-War Japanese Poetry* stand out. Not the least of the factors contributing to this ability was Guest's receptivity to Japanese culture. During his six-year stay in Japan, he immersed himself in the learning of the Japanese language and in the contemporary Japanese poetry scene. The results were life-long friendships, the gathering of new forms and images to enrich his poetry, and a ground-breaking anthology of post-war Japanese poetry. 'Heritage and Peril' concludes: "Words belong to poets. We should not let them be handed over to commercialism, triviality, dishonesty and waste." Guest's own poetry and his translations more than justify these words.

Harry Guest

Heritage and Peril

Poetry occurs in both space and time. Whether we read a poem on our own or hear it recited, the experience deepens in time as we follow the sense from beginning to end. This experience also occurs in space because each poem—even *The Iliad* after it was written down—exists as an *objet*. Ronsard's sonnets differ from Shakespeare's—the former are divided into octave and sestet (we see the gap and appreciate its importance as the last six lines introduce a new concept complementing or in some cases challenging the first eight) whereas the latter have three quatrains followed by a rhyming couplet rounding off the central argument. We cannot ignore the unconscious effects of the visual *look* of any poem.

According to Horace a poem ought to be a picture (*ut pictura poesis*). He believed that a poem, rather than being abstract, should depict reality rationally like a Roman painting. This has interesting implications for the composers of concrete poetry since, at first glance, a concrete poem seems to exist only in space not time. However, in his *Agape and Eros* for example, Niikuni uses the character for "attract" as a centre and splits its sections north, south, east and west to make a punning statement: "language is bound to the heart in love". The eye takes notice of these relationships in *time* while admiring the created shape in *space*.

Concrete poetry's greatest strength may be the way it communicates internationally. Even if you don't understand Portuguese, you can comprehend a poem by L.C. Vinholes with the minimum of verbal equivalents. Concrete poetry plays with the relationship between various components. Once you've grasped the meaning plus the pure sound of each individual component you are able to put them together to see a different whole. Such an interpretation of concrete poetry relies on the eye's movement among the pieces of information shown to weave a spider's web of connections in time, arising from the apparently static effect of each picture-poem in space.

No investigation into the development of concrete poetry can ignore Lewis Carroll. James Joyce, surprised by their strange quality, did not read his books as if they had been directed at children. Many of Carroll's experiments with jokes, puns, and the logic of fantasy and "portmanteau" words (for example "slithy" from "lithe" and "slimy") anticipate twentieth-century practice. The Surrealists acknowledged him as their predecessor, appreciating the way he arranged disparate elements and justified irrationalism rationally. Cocteau's late poems *Clair-Obscur* are based on Carroll's use of chiaroscuro and in several of his films (*Le Sang d'un poète* and *Orphée* for example) the world on the other side of the poet's mirror on the screen echoes the world of Alice's chess-board on the page. To-day's concrete poets are also indebted to Carroll's individual use of typography: the gnat in *Through the Looking-Glass* speaks in extremely small letters, the title and the entire first line of *Jabberwocky* are printed in mirror-type (it is a mirror-world after all!) and, in *Alice in Wonderland,* when the mouse embarks on a long *tale,* Alice alters what she hears into a long *tail* so the mouse's thinning appendage crawls across and down the page foreshadowing Apollinaire's *Calligrammes.*

Concrete poetry can also be traced back to the orchestral arrangement of Mallarmé's *Un Coup de dés.* There, the capitalised themes co-operate in counterpoint (sometimes in parallel) with the other themes in lower case. The poem is a vast musical experiment resembling an operatic score wherein several motifs keep criss-crossing in time and space. The words and sentences are visual but, of course, exist shot through with meaning. Chassé believed that the definition of each word in *Littré* would provide the key to Mallarmé's individual (and obscure) usage. Even if Mallarmé intended words to act as music, it would be a mistake to think that such "music" was the precursor of the "pure sound" poetry of Hugo Ball, Kurt Schwitters or Bob Cobbing.

Poetry, by reason of its existence on the printed page, is close to an ornamental art. If we forget that man is *homo ludens* we will no longer create poems for the sake of sound, shape, colour, movement—for pure enjoyment. *Play* is a necessity for life. Norman McClaren's *Blinkety Blank*, Duchamp's *Fountain* and Garnier's typography serve as examples. Dismissing convention they went on to innovate. For pleasure, irony and challenge.

However, it is vital not to ignore precision in the case of artistic creativity. Writing poetry is to create images or perhaps the structure connecting the images. The expression "art for art's sake" is often cited but there is a danger that doctrines, theories, and -isms can lead us away from life, so that the important business of *communication* is ignored. Words would be left to the grammarians' dissection of dead words, the professional inaccuracy of politicians and the superficiality of advertising. Words belong to poets. We should not let them be handed over to commercialism, triviality, dishonesty and waste.

[The original English text is lost. Andrew Houwen translated Niikuni Seiichi's Japanese version published in ASA, volume 4 number 4 and Harry Guest has cleared up a few of Niikuni's understandable misreadings of his text in the 1970 magazine.]

Peter Jay

Nerval's 'Fantasy'

Harry's poetry, which I've enjoyed for more than forty years, has not had its public due, although it has had notable admirers—the late Michael Hamburger, for one, often mentioned how good he thought Harry was. He was talking just of his English poetry. And like Hamburger, Harry may have contrived to become better known as a translator for inventing a new poet with an original and compelling voice: Harry Guest's Victor Hugo. His re-imaginings of Hugo's poems read as if freshly and originally written in English—which, of course, they were.

You could liken the role of translator to one half of a joint venture, the original poet being the other: a sleeping partner, one might say, since he has invested so much in the enterprise and does not intervene. Against the odds—nineteenth-century poetry being notoriously difficult to re-tune as modern English—Harry has negotiated with Victor Hugo a wonderful "English" poet. And there is reciprocity; you are drawn back to Hugo's French both for itself, and to see how Harry has treated it, how he could possibly have managed his transformations.

I wanted to salute Harry's achievement with something French, and chose a poem which I've long liked and long thought harder to translate than a superficial look might suggest. (If something is easy to translate, it's probably not worth doing; but if it's hard ... well, then you call it 'impossible'.)

So this Gérard de Nerval poem is my homage to Harry, and to the generation of Victor Hugo too. Gérard was by six years Hugo's younger contemporary. I may be wrong in thinking that this poem, first published in 1832 when he was twenty-four, has an air of exercise (at least from the technical point of view) about it. It has an untroubled, even a light (is that an illusion?) feel, but certainly prefigures many of his recurrent themes and symbolic images. And it was not at all easy for me to try to translate. I claim little credit for the version other than as a shuffler of phrases and synonyms, having despaired of fuller or more exact, more musical assonance and rhyme, and knowing that translating a single poem is nothing like taking on a whole *oeuvre* or a substantial selection from a prolific giant such as Hugo.

Fantaisie

Il est un air pour qui je donnerais
Tout Rossini, tout Mozart, tout Weber,
Un air très vieux, languissant et funèbre,
Qui pour moi seul a des charmes secrets!

Et, chaque fois que je viens à l'entendre,
De deux cents ans mon âme rajeunit …
C'est sous Louis treize; et je crois voir s'étendre
Un coteau vert, que le couchant jaunit,

Puis un château de brique à coins de pierre,
Aux vitraux teints de rougeâtres couleurs,
Ceint de grands parcs, avec une rivière
Baignant ses pieds, qui coule entre des fleurs;

Puis une dame, à sa haute fenêtre,
Blonde aux yeux noirs, en ses habits anciens,
Que, dans une autre existence peut-être,
J'ai déjà vue … et dont je me souviens!

Gérard de Nerval

Fantasy
for Harry Guest

There is an air for which I'd give away
All of Rossini, Mozart, all Weber,
A very old, a yearning, funeral air,
One which has secret charms alone for me.

And every time I happen to hear that tune,
Two hundred years are taken off my heart …
The time is Louis Thirteenth; I see rolled out
A green hill, yellowed by the setting sun,

Then a brick castle with corners built of stone,
Its panes of glass stained in reddish hues,
Encircled by great gardens, with a stream
Lapping its feet, as it runs among the flowers;

Then at her lofty window she appears,
Fair with black eyes, dressed in antique style,
The lady whom in another life perhaps
I have already seen … and recognize!

Translated by Peter Jay

Peter Josyph

harry-san

mr. moto and
harry-san fly from that old
mt. fuji in snow

it's a great leap like
any other—not for you
not for me—*for them*

no strain involved—puh
strain'd kill these winter men
worrying the air

higher than the wind
looking down on birds of such
meager altitude

macarthur wanted
to give it a grey mushroom
(level it for show)

waste of gadgetry
when harry and mo can bring
it down with a leap

leap to leave these laws
of serizawa science
fly in every face

venture out of that
primal soup of drunkenness
gossip, etc.

(no use for newton's
principia cept to raise
you when the seat's low)

escape these wars down
here, up there, not me, who're
you, mate?—uh—enough

float above *all* those
bashō miles… *all* that haiku
slavery to shrines…

temples of zen war-
men blinded by visions of
samurai heroes…

random rites of spring
as hiroshima sidewalks
blossom atomic…

float above that old
floating world even. mo say
"harry-san have *lift*"

lift like lift of shake
the black sesame, brew the
green matcha ink—*lift*

like boil the red rice
like you can leave your horse at
home harry, hmm? *lift*

like monsieur hugo
house guest rises reciting
like an englishman

mo says: "not all welsh-
man struck to ground fail flesh-test
bull-throated stone-man...

welsh harry made for
brave-like tramp-er-ing above...
master cloud-runner...

master lift-over...
master light-note... master fleet-
through-snow-tokyo"

just don't expect to
hear them in london on the
secrets of fuji

something was heard once
yet to be translated in
rue visconti sure

and a draft came down
the mountain this year but it
was avalanched—*boom*

tank man shakes his head:
insouciant. maybe that
slut-girl knows—so what?

(no place the same for
more than a minute—neither
is a man, harry

you're an event, mo's
an event, and I'm... well... I'm
alfred north whitehead)

peter-san has yet
to hear a word. some secrets
have a loyalty

loyal to what keeps
you in the air... loyal to
what sings the sun up...

loyal to pleasing
jean cocteau... loyal to what's
burning in the glass...

loyal to naming
that flower correctly (*one*
of us needs to know)...

loyal to letting
the night go dark when there's too
much light again—*look*

mr. moto glides
the empty chair, sits in smoke
sips the cold black mud

harry-san places
that word after this in that
old fuji notebook

sees himself in mo's
kurosawa glasses like
the farthest of men

what's the talk at this
table? cup on saucer, pen
on paper breathing

Peter Josyph

PHILIP KUHN

all over a bier in falkensee

4 harry

kein kluger Streiter hält seinen Feind gering
(Goethe)

if i tell you   that its   THE   // terror   of the
      faux amis / the *falsche freunde*
                        (but not ALL *falsaj amikoj*
                            / *mi querido amigo*)
   like *decepcións* carried on the back of those that
arrive unbidden   on the verge of a   sudden mo
ment of *hapuningu* /   ハプニング
    (which   is   or was to say the meaning/s of in
comprehen/ sibles   as *grunnio* was / is
                   as green   as word-worts dancing
                           quick-slo-mo
  with all her fickle friends whose threads of love blossom
not in semiotic flower   but through twisting
        shifting succulent fruiting
    but too sour for my sweet taste is not yet *sensibile* to her *sayonara*
  intoxicado perfume   ) since all her *gifts*   have
  persuaded me to swifter strokes / of *volubile* illocution
  with their *prati-svaras* whispering & *syand*
humming in *pra-moda* love of lovers evading letters
          whilst fading through that *fictus* impress of
    all impos/sibilities

so when i tell you   that it was
          (*übersetzbarkeit* / *oder die möglichkeit*)
  not the leaf that has fallen from the angels of a shoulder
    not the garial whose sounds resound in the silence of *der* Kiefer
not even the in *compréhensifs* / BUT her perfidious lovers who tipped me *pra*
        over the reichenbach
              falls

      those cruel imposters creeping in cold freddo summer-nights like
  barmen babbling *nirabbuda* words in
hubble-bubble sounds // their hugger-mugger whorls slung / over gibberts
    so knotted that i heard them only as a *bribe*
      skulking in the silhouette of shadows
          glistening from her knife

legend
decepción = a disappointment [Spanish]
hapuningu = an unexpected occurrence, a surprise [Japanese]
grunnio = grunt like a pig [Latin]
sensibile = sensitive [Italian]
sayonara = if that be so; goodbye [Japanese]
intoxicado = poisoning [Spanish]
gift = poison [German]
volubile = changeable, fickle [Italian]
prati-svaras = echo [Sanskrit]
syand = trickle down [Sanskrit]
pra-moda = excessive joy, delight [Sanskrit]
fictus = false [Latin]
der Kiefer = jaw, jawbone whereas die Kiefer = pine (tree, wood) [German]
compréhensifs = compassion; an understanding friend [French]
pra = an habitual term applied to persons or things of special sanctity or
              dignity [Burmese]
freddo = cold [Italian]
barmen = to moan or grumble [German]
nirabbuda = a vast number; free from boils or tumours [Pali]
bribe = a fragment of bread, music or conversation [French]

philip kuhn

Ann Leaney

Poeta nascitur non fit

Most people contributing to this *Festschrift* will know Harry better than I. However, I am probably one of the few to have known him in his early years. It was not until I read his poem 'Autobiography' that I realised—"This is my friend Harry, amazing!" I thought to myself that there must have been something in the air of Beresford Road, Cheam to have made the two of us love poetry. Harry has become a major poet; I myself contribute to magazines in a minor way. I always have my poetry books at hand for leisure reading.

After not meeting Harry for over forty years I found myself on an Exeter doorstep. In my hand was a large bottle of home-made damson gin. Perhaps uppermost in my mind were words of Horace—"No verse can give pleasure for long, nor last, that is written by drinkers of water". When a welcoming Lynn opened the door the bottle dropped from my nervous hands, a ruby red tide spreading everywhere. Groan! Once rescued from this unfortunate start it was lovely to chat for a few hours. Since then we have kept in touch. Happiness is the overriding memory of those years in Beresford Road, just before the start of World War II. Harry and I were the same age and were good companions.

I would like to recall one incident out of many from those days. Harry and I were standing by my father's rockery, in my back garden, one summer afternoon. Harry looked at the nasturtiums on the rockery and said that his father considered nasturtiums to be weeds. Soon we were snipping off the flower heads with nail scissors, Harry having gone home to get an additional pair. Later, regarding a big pile of flower heads we were filled with a glow of satisfaction at having completed a helpful task. The glow did not last for long as on my father's return from work it appeared that he was not altogether appreciative of our efforts. I can remember wailing, "But Harry's father says that nasturtiums are weeds."

To conclude… Years ago I received a card from Harry, in mid-December. The card said that he was taking Lynn to Venice for Christmas. Wow! I was so impressed! That is just what a poet SHOULD do. So, Harry, warmest congratulations from my husband John and myself, not only on your poetry but on reaching the milestone of your eightieth birthday.

Harry Guest

His footsteps took him far. In early days
The East for him was paramount. Inspired,
The ancient gardens turned to words, took root.
And for him, always, there was Italy.
The laser ray, the whiteness and the light
Of Venice. Deep within the walled hill towns
The poet found exquisiteness of place.
Halfway towards the west the swifts still scream
Above red earth and mediaeval stone…
There is a certain richness here where love
Of scholarship, as in the past, obtains.

Tony Lopez

Reading Harry Guest

In 1928 T.S. Eliot wrote, "Pound is the inventor of Chinese poetry for our time". He meant of course that Pound's translations had completely changed the way that Chinese poetry was understood and offered new insights into a civilisation relatively unknown. Pound was a remarkable unconventional translator who incorporated aspects of what he saw in Eastern aesthetics into his own experiments in poetry. This breakthrough was perhaps the most important dimension of modernism in poetry: the foregrounding of the visual aspect in poetic composition, the streamlining of poetic language and focus on the image, and the modernist aesthetic of less-is-more, all of this can be identified in what Pound learned, via his reading of Ernest Fenollosa, when translating from Chinese.

In the later twentieth century, a whole range of English language poets followed this orientation to the East, poets from throughout the English speaking world have engaged with Eastern cultures, with Chinese and Japanese graphic poetries, with the *Yi Jing* and with Zen Buddhism. The results of this international phenomenon have been very mixed; one example that repays careful attention is the poetry of Harry Guest, a brilliant translator poet who knows Japan through living and working there.

My exhibit is a 1960s double poem by Harry Guest from his book *The Cutting-Room*, published by Anvil Press in 1970.

Two Poems for O-Bon
(the Buddhist festival of the Dead; midsummer)

one

Clean the altars.
          Scour
the wood remembering
dead next of kin.
            Their ashes
are gathering energy, emit to love
remembered presences.
           Let
the temple-bell vibrate.

Clean the altars.
         Prepare
the past, a welcome for the past.

And, waiting, pray.

             The ghosts
enter the garden. Familiar
features take shape on the
lamplit leaves.

A sad season (clean,
the altars; longing so,
the garden): chill
inside drab heat.

         Make
the whole house an expectation, greeting
the long-lost and the brief-loved.

Who, lightly, blur
the polished wood of the altars:
departing,
move like the faint

Tony Lopez

shadow of rain across the lanterns,
among us if they ever were
no more again.

   two
             Half-seen
smiles unmet like mist,
maybe the touch of a hand
resembles dew,
their footprints tentative
cobwebs on the grass.

              Spectres
in air-conditioned
cinemas and, suddenly,
footless, shimmering on to the stage.
Tales of melancholy love,
revenge, the green flame
signifying presence.

             Phantoms
hiding behind peonies,
dissolving to hard
bones the further side
of tombstones at rendezvous.

The first poem begins by presenting ritual events in language: the phrases might be instructions to the reader or interior phrases addressed to the speaking self who is carrying out or watching what must be a well-known ceremony. This could be the memory of a familiar ceremony re-enacted in the imagination as it is remembered, and the meaning of the actions, both the emotional significance and the cultural significance, is explored by means of these stepped and carefully spaced lines in which the simple sentences are set out. "Clean the altars" feels like a straightforward instruction, whereas the next three lines "Scour / the wood remembering / dead next of kin", already move from a physical task to the mental activity that accompanies it. The dead relatives are now reduced to ash, but that ash is imagined "gathering energy" as if in some sense active if not fully alive. Of course the altar wood, which is being scoured for the ceremony, is connected with firewood and ash; there is a suggestion that the wood, as well as the person who scours it, remembers the "dead next of kin". The sentence that signals a particular, and for the reader, an imaginary sound (the vibrating temple-bell) has been separated into two parts by a line break after the verb. This pattern of isolating the initial verb is repeated as a structure throughout the poem: "scour", "let", "prepare", "make", are thus separated out as beginning verbs and 'pray' is also isolated by the very particular eisthesis of long indents after the line breaks. The indents allow notional lines to be completed so that the *mise-en-page* is opened and spread out, similar in appearance to verse drama exchanges and many passages in Pound's later *Cantos*. The spacing is a set of implied reading instructions, incorporating pauses, adding emphasis to the verbs, and slowing down a performance of the poem.

The verse is managed and punctuated mainly by means of line breaks but the sentences are also reinforced as units, separated in every case by a long indent pause, sometimes extended by a clear line space. I think the verse shape is a sympathetic attempt to construct a re-enactment of the O-Bon ritual in language, to give the stages of the ceremony their due respect. The phrase "clean the altars" is repeated, twice used as a separate sentence with space around it, and once located within a bracketed aside that is itself within a blocked four-line indented sentence. But the third instance of the phrase is a variation "clean, the altars" meaning the altars are now clean. The repeated and varied phrase within the pattern of instructions is what gives the poem its ritual quality. But the spacing pattern is not continued right through the poem. There is a turn after the line "And, waiting, pray." This is the point at which the poem becomes supernatural as "The ghosts / enter the garden."

In its second half the first poem's line breaks are hard returns to a steadier more solid left hand margin and the long indent is used only once with the blocked indent passage (beginning "A sad season") interposed within the break. In this half the insubstantial presence of the familiar dead is tactfully imagined as a sequence of indefinite and uncertain images: as shapes seen among leaves, as a light blur on polished wood, as a shadow of rain across lanterns. They are ghosts; they are "the long-lost and the brief-loved" that are accommodated within that figure of opposition (long / brief – lost / loved) and in the imagined garden only on a temporary basis. This is not a Buddhist poem exactly—it certainly would not need its parenthetical subtitle if it were—but it is a respectfully thoughtful poem about a Buddhist custom, imaginatively working through the implications of the ceremony it describes.

The second poem is linked structurally to the second half of the first poem in that it presents images of the familiar dead within each of its three stanzas or verse paragraphs. Now the ghosts are imagined through insubstantial smiles, touch, footprints, compared in the first stanza with natural phenomena: mist, dew, and cobwebs on wet grass. In the second stanza the scene changes to a cinema and the spectres seem to be made equivalent to ghosts. The reader will imagine ghosts on screen, as in a supernatural movie, or recognise that filmic characters are ghosts of a sort.

But in the heat of midsummer Japanese people like to go to the cinema to watch horror films of traditional ghost stories to cool down. And in the Kabuki theatre, ghost characters have no feet; they have long gowns that hide the actors' feet and move with short steps, appearing to glide. A green light is the theatrical signal whenever a ghost is on stage. In the third stanza "phantoms" are seen behind peonies, presumably identified with the lush beautiful heads of garden flowers, growing among tombstones and bones.

The ghosts are allowed to come provisionally and temporarily into a garden (and into a poem) set up for this ceremony that honours the dead. They are given space and time and then seen to be gone "among us if they ever were / no more again". In a sense the ceremony uses the superstition of the returning dead to be rid of them the rest of the time. The ceremony, at least as it is portrayed here, is a framework for the living to give proper respect to, and thus be free of the dead and the associated fear, guilt and remorse, for the rest of each year.

I suppose that we should read this poem as a special kind of anthropological text, which takes a common Buddhist religious custom and makes it available to a Western readership. No one is going to deliberately seek out and use this text to find out about Buddhism. Poetry allows elements of the custom to be recomposed in a precision-made English text that encodes finely discriminated shades of insubstantial and ambiguous meaning. The equivocation over the presence of ghosts allows the possibility of a spiritual dimension, without any dogmatic statement of belief. This is tactful and delicate writing. Of course it is not intending to be anthropology in the sense of responsible social science but it is rather concerned with imaginative sympathy, with the representation of emotional and psychological being in its proper complexity. The poem does depend, however, on the O-Bon custom being unfamiliar, on the report coming from a faraway land, and it instates Guest as an experienced traveller reporting back to his western readers.

'Two Poems for O-Bon' appears in a book, *The Cutting Room*, whose wrap-around cover design is composed of Japanese characters set in long vertical lines printed in grey on off-white as a background to the author's name and title, also set vertically in red upper case type. There is an outline square, type high, between the name and the beginning of the title. The English letters in Roman type, still legible running vertically down the page, but seen sideways on, relate in the design to the fainter vertical lines of Japanese characters, and the red outline square enhances this visual connection. The back cover copy tells us that "Harry Guest's second book contains his poems written in Japan during 1967-9" and explains that "the cover shows a detail of the Japanese translation by Eiji Yamazaki of 'A Bar in Lerici' by Harry Guest".

The whole design and presentation of the book relates Harry Guest's experience of Japan and writing about Japan with his originality as a poet. The use of Japanese characters on the cover incorporates a Japanese visual aesthetic into the book as a whole and has a similar effect to that of Pound incorporating Chinese characters into the Cantos. The cover concept incidentally informs us that Guest is an international figure whose poem about Italy, translated by a Japanese poet, is published in Japan. The first poem in the collection is 'December in Kagoshima' set in a famous Japanese tourist spot that is being visited out of season. In the book there are family poems and various kinds of love poems, including the extended and ambitious sequence 'Metamorphoses' that is, in its sexual frankness, helping to establish the new freedoms of that time. Some of this writing is located in, or contains descriptive elements of, Japanese landscape and culture. The reader comes across maples, banana trees, rice-fields, volcanoes, bamboos, palms, orange trees, typhoons, and Japanese names such as Kagoshima and O-Bon. But these are the incidental details of a cultural pluralism that is the unifying idea of the book as a collection. 'Two Poems for O-Bon', with its generous and imaginative presentation of identity and difference, and its openness to spiritual experience, is at the centre of this theme. Guest's poem, which takes up the Poundian method of clearing space around carefully-placed images, seems also to manifest a similar ambition to that of the early Pound writing *Cathay*, introducing us to another world with a different aesthetic and a different framework of belief.

Tony Lopez

A Detailed Version   *For Harry*

Near this building are two exhausted men and a bundle of provisions.
The generic space represents the structure shared by the inputs.
On the right, tracts and nuclei are shown in black.
The seated woman wears a Hudson's Bay Company trade blanket that
    cost four beaver skins.
Proximity to the main road makes the tower a target for graffiti.

If you can see the entire room in detail, you've got some tightening up to do.
Wang Lü climbed Mt Hua in 1381.
The most useful imagery for vegetation mapping is band 7 or a false
    colour composite.
Collectors in Lancashire noticed a surge in the frequency of dark individuals.
Page 200 is not part of this preview.

Experiments were performed at room temperature.
Each dot represents one individual pair.
Maturity will occur on any anniversary if eight of the ten shares are equal
    to or greater than their opening levels.
When you're finished, the animation should appear fluid and smooth.
Output measures identify problems but not the nature or cause.

This list is an example.
During the game, information flows between the service front end and
    web services.
Cahun's registration card tracks her journeys to and from Jersey until her
    death in 1954.
One of the crew has a bright blue shoulder bag labelled LOOK OUT.
A screen on the seatback assumes binocular vision.

Steel rods or mesh are put into the mould.
Number 7, now the Georgian House Museum, was built for John Pinney
    who owned sugar plantations on Nevis in the Caribbean.
The address is a basic unit of identity but it can take a variety of forms.
This is a more detailed version.
If he comes across an unpainted road, he paints it.

Rupert M. Loydell

'Ultimate translator not working and can't be fixed'
for Harry Guest

Here's the first in a series of guest posts.

Currently we're recruiting for a translator
to register for work with us for the upcoming drama.
It's a familiar story which a million manners salute.

Hi. I would like to be a tester of your translation.
What a great honour for me with large price to make
products that stand up to the punishing environment.

But if that were as these translator's functionings
we would be doomed to extinction more elaborate.
There exists there an ambition between best

to other circumstances. Target language
involves rewriting the sickness of gobbledygook
on the basis of texts I riddle most recent.

I wishes what publishes more other people's experiences
so am looking for psychological prosperity of agreements
and employees digging out dramatic heft and dignity.

I was thoroughly tickled by question in approximate English
the flood which bound havoc to its writers of society
imposed by diagonal alliteration of 'guest' and 'glory'.

As winter grows rough with more heavy frost severe
a person who has become now is given hospitality
to receive creative tales via means of headphones.

If everything is fine it is an opportunity to oblige
a large means of special resource with dedicated information.
I know his words to have found to hope move and very you also.

Boathouse, Early Morning
after Ivon Hitchens

The sky lifts a veil
from right to left,
shadows awry.

A boat swings:
splashed focus
on dark water.

It is hardly day.
The first cloud
scuds into light,

trees hold themselves
upright against a
scribbled mustard dawn.

The scene is frozen
in warmth; matt olive,
stained ochre, reds.

The colours themselves
about to break
into daylight,

the still lake
soon to teem
with life.

John Mingay

Arrangements

I lie inside the night
noting my own disintegration
and a future
where we had arranged to meet again.

Radiance is where
sense is, you are.

I brush
off frequent petals
beneath the silence of the bright cascade
we had begun.

You assume
the right responses to each act.

Soon, knowledge of you will out-cancel pain.

Some Times

We can
push
the door
open

careful
no tear
of theirs
should
shine
uninfected
with duplicity

unaware
of future
of haze
and uncertainty.

We can
hear
the scrape
of textures

ink-smeared words

anyway:

each
to test
interpretations
of the lost—

a wrongness
in the atmosphere.

Still

as
unpredictably
as fingerposts
to scribbled lies
in lieu
of whereabouts
which now
matter less
than ever

in their
autumn state
they don't own
reality…

transmuted
one key-moment
caught:

for only we
can know
why it's hard
to hold the past
in place
using
a rope of fog.

These poems were constructed using lines selected from the Harry Guest books that gave them their titles. They are offered to Harry on the occasion of his 80th birthday with gratitude and much respect. Written: Dunfermline, Fifeshire, January to March 2012.

John Mingay

John Mingay

It's Hard to Hold the Past in Place Using a Rope of Fog.
A review of Harry Guest's *Some Times*

I first came across Harry Guest's poetry around thirty years ago with his 1968 Anvil book *Arrangements*. Since then, I've continued to read him and have regularly used his work to illustrate various poetic techniques wherever I've taught. In 1996, I even had the privilege of publishing his *Visit to an Unknown Suburb* as a Raunchland chapbook.

But why do I mention all this? Quite simply to declare an interest that may have a bearing on what follows.

And, given this interest, then, it's easy to understand the sense of excitement I felt when I pulled his latest book, *Some Times*, from the envelope. Could he, at nearly eighty, still pull it off? Could he still demonstrate the same ability to innovate and experiment? Or had age taken the edge off what he had to say and the ways in which he said it?

The short answer, I'm delighted to report, is yes he could, yes he could and no it hasn't. The poems in this collection are unmistakably Guest's—warmly human, intelligently considered, measuredly joyful, abundantly evocative and, without pandering in the least to the current, odious trend for dumbing-down, readily accessible. Yet, there's also evidence of him not having stopped developing, of having continued to search for new ways to express the new themes he wants to express.

At Harry Guest's stage of life it's perhaps permissibly inevitable that he admits to the overriding theme in *Some Times* as being memory and the tricks it plays. Much of what he has included is retrospective in flavour. But why not? He's got many years' worth of happy, confusing, sad and celebratory experiences to draw on. However, that's not to say that it's in any way sentimental. Even the section, *Beyond the Rim*, containing poems for the dearly departed, refuses to fall into the grip of slushiness. Instead, Guest fills them with life.

> You stay in memory
> as generous and unaffected, your talk
> glinting with merriment, your work
> inventive, knotty, scrupulous.
>   [from 'Thom Gunn 1929-2004']

Guest has a way of making so much of what he writes read as though it is a stream of consciousness, fresh and idiosyncratic. He is an observer, a reporter who allows the reader the space to interpret—nothing is crammed down the throat—it can simply be read or, for the more adventurous, delved into to uncover the layers of meaning.

> …simpler than mere witnessing
> though easier as always
> to set down than decipher
>
> [from 'Duloe']
>
> We drive to our hotel past hoardings advising
> a foreigner whom to vote for, explaining
> why banks love to dish out money, proving
> how hair-spray makes a goddess, offering
> sly tips for the timeliest bargains
> and prophesying when each one of us
> will get the golden fruit that is our due.
>
> [from 'Palindrome: The Loire Valley']

In continuing to innovate, Guest has taken the stream of consciousness concept to its extreme with 'As Far as Angkor Wat' in which the punctuation even becomes part of the flow of words…

> what's been derived from yellowed pamphlets helps
> only in part dash even photographs
> must cheat because you have to pace the thing
> out for yourselves and sense uneven steps
> comma a mediaeval play of sun
> down far symmetric cloisters comma see
> firsthand the blackening waste of rain along
> those crumbling arcades full stop

Of course, you might think that, after seventy-four lines, a feature of this type might become a little tiresome. But, no. Quite the reverse. It adds to it, providing timing to the cadences without having to interrupt the current of diction. You might think it would appear forced or manufactured. But, no. Quite the reverse. It adds to it, providing a quirkiness that makes it all the more interesting. Anyway, that, in essence, is another feature of Guest's work—nothing is forced. There's none of the forcing of terminology or name-dropping that others indulge in. With Guest, if it's the right word, it goes in. And it goes in without jarring.

> ...still ponds
> mirrored pewter
> smudges along
> the threatened sky
> while smoke drifted
> from one unseen
> cottage which could
> boast yellow walls
> not to say a
> gaudy muster
> of hollyhocks
> to interrupt
> the going scheme.
>
> [from 'The Poetry of Ideas']

So, when all's said and done, this collection really holds no disappointments, not even to a seasoned Guest-reader like me, and goes to show he can still pull it off, splendidly, right through to the Meldrewesque ire of 'An Open Letter to Librarians with Closed Minds', a selection of translations of the likes of Verlaine, Haufs and Serafini, and the pathos of a sequence of love poems looking back on a relationship that became 'unclasped without a wan pretence / of plagency'.

I certainly hope I have more opportunities in the years ahead to pull many other new collections from Harry Guest from their envelopes. His will be a hard act for anyone to follow.

Bob Nash

Umbrian Odyssey

Harry was a colleague for thirty years, and has been a close friend for forty years. As the former he accompanied us on A-Level Art History visits to Italy, inspiring the students with his knowledge and feeling for Italian art and culture.

He has a great—catholic—interest in the visual arts in that he loves both classical art and modern—he has a wide appreciation and knowledge of Rothko's work for example. This erudition is shown in his 2000 publication *The Artist on the Artist*, a book that I believe should be on the lists of all students who are contemplating study in the Humanities. Harry has often said to me how much he admires artists and wishes he could paint, but in his response to modern painting; the pleasure he draws from it; and the re-charging effect to his sensibilities it has had from his continuous gallery visits shows in his poetry. We have had many visits with him to theatre and film, both of which he is enthusiastic and knowledgeable. He knows more about W.C. Fields than most.

After having taken groups of students to Italy over the years, when we both retired we arranged, the four of us, to spend some time in that special country. So we rented a gîte in Umbria near Lake Trasimeno; central for all the art centres of that wonderful region.

We put the car on the train to Nice to motor on from there. Leaving the couchette next morning we were treated to a scene which augured well for anyone interested in art. From the corridor we looked across the French landscape to see in the distance an escarpment and peak familiar to us—the magnificent Mont St Victoire, of Cézanne.

During the train journey I had a first-hand example of Harry's other great skill—as translator of many languages—in this case, Japanese. Harry had brought an enormous suitcase; too large to put onto the luggage rack; so he had to leave it in the corridor—to the annoyance of two young Japanese travellers, one of whom said (subsequently translated for us by Harry), "Look what some bastard has left here." They were completely nonplussed when Harry (in best Japanese of course) replied, "I'm sorry, I'll move it."

We left the train and breakfasted on Nice Station (both of us thinking of Somerset Maugham passing through the same place in the past). We collected the car and set off across the Rivera east towards the Italian border.

Paddy and I have been privileged to be among those who have had a Harry Guest poem written especially for them. How did this come about? We stopped the next night just near Monte Carlo, and Harry recalled the pleasure of this and its art association to us by remembering a famous painting by Roaul Dufy. The painting captures the essence of carefree leisure of that Mediterranean life, and Harry, in his turn, has captured the essence of that painting. His misgivings mentioned above about wishing he could be a painter are obviated—he has made his poem 'Dufy's Flags' work like a painting.

The culmination of the journey to Umbria took in familiar sites from our past Art History visits, but the arrival at the gîte was spectacular. We arrived after dark to an old cottage in the midst of vineyards. But next morning we were delighted to look across a vista of Umbrian landscape to a distant ridge of hills on which, just visible, we caught a glimpse of that fabulous hill town, Montepulciano, which we would visit. I managed to sketch Harry contemplating that view and expectation.

Congratulations Harry on your eightieth.

Thanks, not only for your great company on the trips, but also for our friendship with you and Lynn over the last four decades, which has been so pleasurable and inspiring.

William Oxley

Over the years in Devon, Patricia Oxley and myself have been involved in making poetry events happen. It should be explained that Patricia does not, herself, write poetry, whereas I do. She brings editorial discrimination to our various projects; and I publish the occasional book of poems. My reward is such publications and a certain input into various poetry live events; hers is being able to share her reader-listener's appreciation of the art with as many people as possible. So my role in these things has been recognized, like I say, by book publication and by helping to shape the various projects; while hers was recognized by the award of an MBE in 2011 'for services to poetry'.

In the early years of the Dartington Ways With Words Festival, and subsequently with the Torbay Poetry Festival, Harry Guest was invited to participate. At the Ways With Words Poetry Day organised by Patricia, he gave a well-received reading of his own poetry. Now, in addition to poetry-event-making, Patricia has edited the literary magazine *Acumen* for the last 27 years. Consequently, there has developed a symbiotic relationship between the written and spoken word through events and the magazine. Harry Guest was an early contributor to *Acumen*, and in that way joined some of our various projects. I should also add that in 1994, the publisher Stride—then based in Harry Guest's home city of Exeter—asked me to edit an anthology of poets whom I felt were either neglected or, at any rate, outside the then current mainstream. This I did, and the anthology was subsequently published under the title of *Completing The Picture*. It included a number of poems by Harry; and here is what I wrote as prefatory note about the poet and his work:

> Born in Wales, 1932, and educated at Malvern College, Worcester, Cambridge University, and the Sorbonne. He expressed the poet's sense of exile well in the lines: "I sit… / brooding on nemesis and fearing / luck… / I write alone and timorous / left contemplating darkness and the sea." Commenting on his own metrical practice he speaks of using "syllables or stress-length lines", with a "high premium on musicality". I don't find his work especially musical, but we'll let that pass; his real strength lies, as Howard Sergeant—his first publisher—observed, in 'skilfully manipulated images and

association of ideas'. Guest began publishing his poetry in the 1960s—that decade of confusion in most things, including the craft of verse—and spent six years in Japan, before coming home to immerse himself in teaching in the provinces. The phrases "a big fish in a little pond", and "a well-known name in obscurity" spring readily to mind to account in part for Harry Guest's relative neglect, despite regular publication. That, and the following of a rather erratic trajectory in his poetry from the relatively traditional approach in his earliest work, via a period of Sixties' avant-gardism, to a reversion to the earlier style in more recent years, with the added bonus that feeling—the essential ingredient of all poetry—has begun to displace the more austere diet of ideas and imagism. There seems to be also, according to the editor of *Acumen* magazine, "a latent narrative tendency which has yet to fully realise itself in his verse".

What that critical note ignored was, of course, the poet's considerable presence in the field of poetic translation. However, his participation in the 9th Torbay Poetry Festival symposium on translation, and the subsequent conversion of his paper, and those of his fellow translators Timothy Adès, Fred Beake and Martin Sorrell, into an 'Interview With Four Translators' published in *Acumen* 68, rectified the omission. His replies in the interview were both seriously revealing about the art of translation as, for example, when he quoted his own words from a 2009 Shearsman volume, "for me 'the effort of translating is a vital complement to creative writing, providing not only a technical challenge but also the strange effect of inhabiting another's consciousness for a while'."; and amusing, as when I asked him, "as a poet in his own right", had he found it financially more lucrative to do translation work than publish his own poetry? His reply was, "It is always a pleasant surprise to get paid for my work! I suppose over the years they've evened out. Not lavishly!"

One does not have to read too far into Harry's work to detect his genial disposition. And that has been my experience of the man himself. Consequently, I would like to dedicate this poem of mine about Richard Hooker, another great Exeter luminary, to Harry on the occasion of his 80th birthday:

Ecclesiastical Polity
(For Harry Guest)

His statue is thoughtful, bookish, grey
                           but not grave
in the green cathedral close. Beneath the
                           great gaze
of holy history, Richard Hooker ponders
                           genially
as an August evening turns the massed
                           frontage
to a cliff of shine. And the saints
                           look down
upon the man who justified the ways
                           of Anglicanism
to God, and began the emancipation
                           of prose,
English-prose—shining the light of faith
                           into every
corner of its dark and clotted syntax. Hooker
                           for love,
and Swift for hate, taught
                           the secret
of a living style that is clarity of mind
joined with the subtleties of God.

Alasdair Paterson

Walk beginning and ending with lines by Harry Guest

In Sho's
wild garden irises and a persimmon-tree,
the skyline circled by dark green mountains.

Harry, the valley stores are out
of persimmon and most other things
apart from mutton pies and whisky
and value packs of caramel wafers.
Life expectancy, mysteriously, is surging;
they must be digging for longevity
out in the bungalow plots, under the hills,
between boggy meadows where irises
flourish under another language banner.

Here, up close, the mountain's green
is different every brushstroke, darkened
or lightened by the feud between
pine shadow and rhododendron smother.
I'm past the tree-line, breathing hard,
scuffing the geology at the top
and I'll concede it's harder now
each time I make the climb; I'll have
my work cut out to get back down
before night clatters through the trees.

So I'm hankering for that kind
of pavilion, not even a mansion,
you'll see in oriental painting;
you know the kind of thing, refuge
for poets and sages and painters
and starved souls needing nourishment.
Nothing much but a roof, a bed, a fire
and the verandah for wine-drinking,
for viewing the modulations of green

as the day sinks and moonlight
picks out rock faces and stray trees;
for letting the landscape inside to make
its own geology there, shifting and
abrading, a tug like long time passing;
for picking up the siren song of vertigo
we don't always want to listen to,
but have to hear and fill our pages with.

And after a quiet night, the dawn up
early and scrambling to the valley, there
at the intersection of *solitary* and *lonely*
I'd remember what life I have down there
and how little I can be without my
dearest people; and, yesterday logged
in notebooks and muscles, pack
everything I need to take away.

And starting down among the trees
I might not see again, I'd watch them
ease themselves from the chilly quilt
of darkness, sway gently through
their morning exercises to a broadcast
of bird music that the light fine-tunes,
Harry, that sweetens for another
breath, another day, *this cage of air.*

Michael Power

Poetry reading in Lancing College 1963

The poets assembled by Harry Guest
Left the Headmaster much distressed.

With considerable fervour
Each one in turn declaimed his *oeuvre*.
The aim perhaps—could that be?
To *épater la bourgeoisie*.

Breath was audibly drawn in,
You could have heard the fall of a pin
When the rows of England's middle-class sons
Heard the line about masturbating nuns.

Tim Rice

'The Bible in Cornwall' is one of my favourite Harry Guest poems.

> Where there's life there's sin. We sabotage
> our own attempts at holiness.
> Christ wears a crown of gorse.
> The tin nails are hourly driven home.

I know Cornwall well and Harry puts it better.

I was a very naïve 16-year-old schoolboy at the beginning of the 1960s when Harry Guest arrived at Lancing College. Simple mathematics (which Harry did not teach) tells me that he would have been just 29 at the time, which of course seems ridiculously young to me now. I first saw him as I saw all schoolmasters at that time—however likeable, not as friends but as members of the staff who, when the chips were down, were not on our side. To my juvenile gaze, the teachers had little idea or interest in their charges beyond teaching us, and keeping us in order.

Maybe I exaggerate my lack of sophistication, but not by much. Nonetheless it was Harry who was foremost in showing me that it was perfectly possible (though by no means inevitable) for each side of the classroom divide to see the other as a comrade, a soul mate, a chum—in fact that there was no divide. I trust I would have cottoned on to this obvious fact in a term or two, or at least before I left Lancing, but Harry, because of his genuine passion for a world that was just beginning to change in myriad ways, culturally and politically, accelerated my awareness.

He did this, in my case anyway, not so much through his classes, but for his palpably genuine enthusiasm for what even the least responsive pupil was up to. He once summoned me to see him after a lesson—I nervously expected a rocket for some misdemeanour or display of ignorance—but he merely wished to tell me that he had enjoyed a recording I had made singing a Cliff Richard number. I wrote some appalling teenage lovesick poems for the school magazine and Harry was kind about one of them. He spotted and encouraged several creative talents that were at the school at the time; he knew about Ray

Charles, which he should not have done; he knew about Camus, more predictably, as a result of which I still do.

He was as memorable a schoolmaster as he is a poet, i.e. very.

In the past half century or more I have enjoyed and admired his poetry, crossed paths with him and Lynn in Japan and the West Country and never felt that he was older than 29. But he is, and I am, and if I reach 80 I shall still enjoy his work not because I know him but because he knows us.

Anthony Rudolf

Harry of Hawthornden and Two Other Guests, November 1993

1.
I remember arriving in my car at Hawthornden Castle (near Lasswade, south of Edinburgh) on a cold and snowy November day. I had driven up from London, with an overnight stay at my sister's house in Leeds. I remember my den at the end of the corridor: it was known as Brontë Room, with the names of former monthly residents in a permanent list by the door, as on the staircases of Cambridge colleges. I remember the log fire, the narrow and uncomfortable bed, the little table for my heavy Adler typewriter.

2.
I remember, *ça va sans dire*, my two fellow Hawthornden Fellows, assigned to or requesting that particular month: Harry Guest, whom I already knew, and Peter Josyph, a playwright and author from upstate New York, whom neither of us knew. The castle accepts seven fellows. Four of the rooms remained empty. I do not remember the names of the rooms in which Harry and Peter were ensconced for the duration.

3.
I remember the rules of the house: socialising permitted only at breakfast and in the evenings: pre-dinner sherry, dinner and sitting around in the large and comfortable lounge. I remember that lunch was brought to our rooms on trays. Afternoon tea and biscuits were left on a table in the corridor for us to collect around four o'clock ("On five-o'clockera à quatre heures, nicht wahr Harry?").

4.
I remember that Harry was using pen and paper for drafting poems: ah that distinctive tiny handwriting so familiar from letters, what size was your writing on the blackboard when you were a schoolmaster, Harry? Peter, on the other hand, was already working on a word processor: a play or a novel, I forget. I was preparing the third draft of my first (and last) novel.

5.
I remember that we got on very well. You could say we bonded. It was good that we did, given we were a closed community, word monks for a month. In addition to us, there were the cook, gardener, cleaners and resident administrator, all of whom catered to most of our needs.

6.
I remember that one evening we met the latest owner of Hawthornden Castle, Mrs Drue Heinz, who must be worth at least fifty-seven million pounds. One of the first owners, Drummond of Hawthornden, was himself a poet. The castle's first poet visitor was Ben Jonson who, unlike me, walked there from London along the Great North Road, passing through Finchley, where I live. 1618, two years after Shakespeare's death: I imagine Ben and Drummond drinking wine in the still extant library and talking about the bard. Ben had strong views: "all those loonies who claim that Will didn't write his own plays. Bloody snobs, if you ask me".

7.
I remember that one evening I drove the three of us to Edinburgh— Harry was to give a reading at a Scottish literary centre, Netherbow. First we went to Waterstones on Princes Street where Peter bought and presented us with copies of *Suttree* by Cormac McCarthy, one of his favourite writers. The next evening we went to a famous literary pub, Milnes on Rose Street, once a haunt of top bard, Sorley Maclean.

8.
I remember, one bright November Sunday, the three of us walked to Rosslyn Chapel, perhaps a mile from the Castle. In those pre-Dan Brown days, entry was easy and free. We learned about the apprentice pillar, which gets its name from an 18th century legend involving a master mason who did not believe his apprentice could carve the column without seeing the original in Rome. The master went to Rome. On his return he found that the apprentice had succeeded in achieving the carving. He killed the apprentice. The pillar is the ultimate masterpiece.

9.
I remember pleasant conversations over and after dinner. We regaled each other with tales of our lives and glimpses into the working day.

Harry would talk about his wife Lynn and daughter Tash, and about his working life in Japan, in Exeter and, long ago, at Lancing College, where he was the favourite teacher of David Hare and my brother-in-law Jack Chalkley. Not so long ago, at the Marlborough Gallery, I reintroduced them to each, after half a century.

10.
I remember that one evening I brought down a cassette which my then (estranged) partner had compiled for me, making dark points about my character through her choice of songs. Harry and Peter did their best to help me identify the tracks. I remember a song by Little Feat, 'Dixie Chicken', which I am listening to on Spotify, even as I type this.

11.
I remember that Fellows are required to write something for the visitors' book. My pre-computer "filing system" does not allow me easy access to my old unpublished poems, which is perhaps just as well. On the other hand, maybe the poem is better than I recall. If it turns up in time, I could include it here. Harry too wrote a poem for the book. What did Peter the playwright offer?

12.
I remember discussing with Harry our mutual passion for French poetry and the poets we had translated over the years. I am drafting this text on the Eurostar, en route to Paris where I shall be visiting two of my poets, Yves Bonnefoy and Claude Vigée. H. Guest is a class act. The hail-fellow well-met uniform disguises a conductor whose orchestra contains violins of deep emotion, brass of sophisticated taste, woodwind of educated intelligence.

13.
I remember walking alone, with a sublime landscape as backdrop, by Drummond's stream, well wrapped up against the Scottish winter. I remember driving every weekday to the local pool for my forty lengths and, on the last day, buying presents at a local shop for all the staff. One of the cassettes I sang along to in the car was a Van Morrison collection which included Yeats' 'Before the world was made'.

14.
I remember visiting the late poet Geoffrey Dutton up near Blairgowrie on the last Sunday of our stay, and being walked round his remarkable nine-acre marginal garden, which led to a Menard Press book, *Harvesting the Edge*. I remember telling Harry and Peter about this transformative experience over breakfast the following morning.

15.
I remember thinking, at the end of the month, that my latest draft of the novel was not very satisfactory. I wrote a new coda, which worked as a self-standing piece. Oh well, perhaps it would end up as a short story even if the novel had to be abandoned. I hoped aloud that Peter and Harry were pleased with their castle work. I forget how they replied.

16.
I remember one of the books I took with me: E.P. Thompson's recently published *Witness against the Beast: William Blake and the Moral Law*, which I read at night before my blissful combo of whisky and valium. I remember discovering various local whiskies you could not find in London ("There is no such thing as a large whisky", S. Heaney).

17.
I remember discussing theatre with Peter Josyph and mentioning that one of the few people I knew in that profession was Susannah York. Later he would write a play for her, or was it a film script? I introduced them to each other in London over a drink, when Peter visited with his friend Barbara. Harry and Peter and I have met two or three times over the years during UK visits by Peter. We promised each other that we would meet again at Hawthornden for a second month of work and stuff. 2013 is the twentieth anniversary of our good month together.

Coda
Round number birthdays are, like Lévi-Strauss' characterisation of totems, "good to think with". When a friend reaches eighty, especially within a few weeks of one's own round number (seventy), one can't help wondering what the past will hold in store. I trust that there are years and miles to go before we sleep. Before we sleep.

LAWRENCE SAIL

Another Way to Read Paul Klee *

The joy of little
multiples, tesseræ,
the parts that add up
to more than their sum,
gradus ad parnassum
via terraces of colour—
and to climb is to find
the key to clover
along with other
botanical marvels

Asters that fizz
like catherine wheels,
roses, their hearts
whorls of green shadow
spinning to deeps
dark as any
explored by a poet

And at night, as the violin
conjures a partita,
the nursery letters
left in the toybox
already piled high
with clowns, fish
and cities, combine
in the codes of camouflage,
more ways to keep
the open secret

*cf Harry Guest's poem 'The Sorcerer's Squares *or* One way to Read Paul Klee'

Daniele Serafini

Translating Harry Guest

I met Harry Guest in 1993 at the Exeter Summer School where I was attending a course of English and Harry was lecturing British Literature. I was soon carried away by his talent, his passion and the colloquial depth of his approach to that wonderful subject. We immediately got on well together and had a few exchanges of viewpoints during the rainy mornings of that rather chilly August. At the end of one of his lectures, he read aloud a couple of his poems and that was really love at first sight with Harry's poetry, if I may say so.

I bought one of his books, which I read on the plane flying back to Italy: going through it was a great experience for the elegance, beauty and peculiar atmosphere of those poems. I decided to translate a few of them, which I wanted to submit to *Origini*, an Italian literary magazine, starting with 'Three Poems for October' and from 'Death of a Friendship'. I found that the "incipit" of the first poem gave the idea of a film, presenting an extraordinary "piano sequenza", recalling the last minutes of *The Passenger*, a film by Michelangelo Antonioni. The camera moves very slowly, catching every single detail of a square and later of a room where the main character, performed by Jack Nicholson, is going to be murdered. So does Harry, as a camera, by a meticulous description of the environment and the psychological atmosphere, with the objects, which besides keeping their phenomenal reality, seem to assume also a symbolic function.

This is a beautiful poem to be translated. That opening stream of images and metaphors suits well also the Italian version even if, inevitably, the structure of English, with a lot of monosyllables and bisyllabic words, requires and imposes a new rhythm in a language where words have a different length, with more syllables. By the way, don't we say in Italian and French with a game of words that unfortunately doesn't work in English, that "tradurre è tradire" or that "traduire c'est trahir"(to translate means to betray)?

This is the hard task of any translator: the point is always whether to privilege musicality or the meaning of the lines, when we can't achieve both targets. Just one only example: when Harry writes at the beginning of 'Three Poems for October', "Brown water laps / at the abandoned boathouse", if in the first line I translate "laps" literally ("cerchi") I save the meaning but I lose some deep flavour of the language. What could I do? What did I do? I opted for a bit old fashion noun ("sciabordìo"), which is fairly onomatopoeic and musical and doesn't betray the original meaning. This was a successful attempt, in my opinion, which led me to this conclusion: you have a good translation when you don't realize at all that this or that poem has originally been written in another language.

A number of Harry's poems have been published in the poetry magazine *Origini*, number 21, December 1993, and number 39, December 1999, published by La Scaletta, San Polo di Reggio Emilia. Some of his recent poems have just appeared in the magazine *ALI*, "rivista d'arte, letteratura, idee", edizioni del bradipo, number 8, Lugo, 2012. Three of them were included also in my collection *Luce di confine* (in English, *Half-light* or *Border Light*), published by Mobydick, Faenza, 1994.

Coming to the end of this short and imperfect tribute to Harry Guest I'd like to say that a good translation is most of the times the result of an *act of love,* without which it can really be a hard task. An act of love towards the poet and his/her poetry. Having deeply loved, and still loving, Harry's poems, which I find elegant, meaningful and deep, my job has been relatively easy, also because Harry Guest's good command of Italian supported me very much with correct remarks and helpful advices.

In the very end I'd like to thank him twice: for introducing me to his work which, to some extent, has influenced my writing in the mid '90s, and for giving me the opportunity to have some of my poems translated into English with the same skill and the same talent Harry puts in his poems. Thanks to his generous mastery, now they live a new life in a new light.

Per Harry Guest

    Guarda, non vedi come
la luce sembra anch'essa prigioniera
di questo ottobre superstite
agli affanni dell'estate;
lieve si cela mutando sotto un cielo
che trascolora in grigio madreperla
verso il bosco di faggi, oltre le dune.
    L'autunno screziato volge alla deriva
distilla forme e colori del tuo canto,
esausta s'attarda anche la luce
sulle pareti d'ocra, sulle tue rose.

For Harry Guest

    Look now can't you see the way
The light too seems a captive
Of this October which is all that's left
From the anxieties of summer—
Light kept so lightly hidden, altering
Under a sky that fades to mother-of-pearl
Towards the beechwood, beyond the downs.
    The speckled autumn starts to drift,
Distils the shapes and colours of your song—
The light too lingers, droops fatigued
On walls of ochre, on your roses.

translated by Harry Guest

Martin Sorrell

Harry Guest Translated:
From Coming To Terms: *two poems, three translations*

Et in arcadia ego

Version 1

ou bien ça signifie
que moi innommé moi
os d'abord et puis cendres
dans cette boîte en pierre
une fois à l'instar
des bergers ébahis
dont les doigts réchauffés
savent tracer ces lettres
sculptées ces bergers qui
défilaient à travers
l'Arcadie insoucieux
ensoleillés parmi
la constante harmonie
des abeilles tandis
que les parfums muables
d'olives et de vignes
se tressaient dans la brise

ou bien ça signifie
que moi La Mort moi crâne
souriant moi rôdeur
tenant faux sablier
qui ne manque jamais
moi mesureur moi qui
coupe court moi dont l'ombre
avec ses longues barres
mettra terme à la danse
prise en plein mouvement

embrassade vendange
l'instant où la victoire
semble à portée de main
on me trouve aussi moi
harcelant l'Arcadie

La Mort

Version 2

Ou bien cela signifie
Que moi sans nom moi
Os un moment et puis cendres
Dans cette boîte en pierre
Autrefois tels
Les bergers badauds
Dont les doigts tièdes
Tracent ces lettres sculptées
Bergers qui défilèrent à travers
l'Arcadie insoucieux
Ensoleillés au sein
De l'harmonie soutenue
D'abeilles en même temps
Que la brise tressa les parfums distincts
D'olive et de vigne

Ou bien cela signifie
Que moi Mort moi crâne au rictus
Moi rôdeur arborant faux
et sablier indomptable
moi mesureur
qui coupe court
celui dont l'ombre barrée
abolira la danse
à son apogée
baisers vendange
l'instant où la victoire

semble saisissable
on me retrouvra
moi La Mort
qui parcours l'Arcadie

Liaisons perdues

Sous la ville et le goudron les sentiers
ne mènent plus aux lieux sacrés

De vagues vapeurs suintent dans les brins d'herbe
jusqu'à effacer tout fil directeur

Partout le silence manque
qui surprenne la rumeur du passé

Nul messager ne saura trahir
la révélation des sous-bois

Quand il n'y a personne aux aguets
des rides se déferlent sur le sol

La pellicule ne laissera paraître
cette silhouette qui s'attarde au portail

Des puits profonds, pas goûtés, recouverts,
renferment la mémoire d'étoiles

Peter Southgate

About Harry Guest

I have known Harry Guest since October 1946, when we both started school at Malvern College. At Malvern neither Harry nor I showed any brilliance at sport (with the notable exception that Harry did gain a very high place in the cross-country run from Ledbury to Malvern).

From an early age at Malvern Harry specialised in French and German, whereas I began with studying Classics and Harry was (typically) envious of my reading Homer in the original Greek. I was quite unaware (at the time) of this privilege. However, I soon transferred to Modern Languages, with much encouragement from Harry, and we spent our schooldays together sharing the same study. Apart from his natural friendliness, sociability and sense of humour, I particularly remember Harry's immense (and infectious) enthusiasm for everything, especially culture and the arts and the acquisition of knowledge about them. This enthusiasm must have made him a brilliant teacher. Even as long ago as the Malvern days Harry seemed to have a natural gift for language and an almost photographic memory. I was more interested in the linguistic side of our studies, but Harry would also delve into and thoroughly enjoy the poetry and the literature. I can remember struggling to understand, for example, Thomas Mann's *Tonio Kröger*, whereas Harry appeared to read this difficult German novel without any great problem. I also remember the breadth of Harry's enthusiasm: for example, at his suggestion, we cycled one day to Hereford to see the beautiful cathedral there and its chain library and Mappa Mundi.

In view of his love of poetry in all languages whilst at Malvern, it is no surprise that he became a brilliant poet. However, in no way has Harry ever seemed to be an intellectual snob but always gets on well with people of all types and from all backgrounds. At most, I believe Harry would try (with his enthusiasm) to steer people to an appreciation of the arts.

After leaving school our lives diverged into different paths. However, we have fortunately kept in touch with each other continuously. Harry has kept me apprised of his activities and particularly of his *oeuvres* when they are published. Fortunately I have a number of his publications, the majority signed by him together with a friendly note and sometimes an allusion to our Malvern days. He certainly values his Malvern days, having gratefully dedicated his *Versions* to (*inter alios*) the three Malvern schoolmasters who taught us both French and German. *Versions* is of course Harry's brilliant translation of French and German poetry into beautiful English poetry (including one of his favourites, Rainer Maria Rilke).

From the very beginning Harry has had his own ideas about writing poetry and has (in my view quite rightly) stuck to his approach and not been led aside by convention. In his early works, such as 'Private View', he has shown some homage to convention but here, as in all his subsequent writing, he makes such striking and skilful use of the English language, producing a myriad of images which (to me) are almost like an orchestra.

To take some examples, in 'Private View' his line "With laments for oh the brevity of beauty" is beautiful but also rather heart-rending. In the same collection of poems I find very effective the startling introduction of the electric fire in the lines of a rather dramatic poem:

Dressed and alone apart from the buzz of the electric fire
I start to analyse a Saturday of love.

Harry's *The Artist on the Artist* is a work of great depth which I enjoyed and read with interest, though I have to admit that I (as a layman) did not fully understand parts of it. I think that Harry probably regards this as his "magnum opus" and certainly the amount of work and research which went into its production must have been enormous.

It is natural that, as we approach our 80th birthday, time itself plays upon our thoughts, and Harry's more recent novel *Time After Time* is an amusing sort of semi-autobiography which exemplifies his rather mischievous sense of humour and, on the more serious side, his love of family and friends. It is of particular interest to me, because a number of characters in the novel (including myself) are real people, given pseudonyms, most of which I recognise as they relate to our schooldays.

His time theme has given rise to his recent collection of beautiful poems entitled *Some Times*. In that collection I am very moved by his poems in memory of friends who have died, I am moved and impressed by the effectiveness of his 'Three Word-Sonnets' (each sonnet having one word per line, but thus completing the picture) and I am very much in support of the sentiment (in the poem relating to librarians) behind the lines:

> By putting keyboards where there should be books
> you sabotage what you've been paid to do.

The thick volume *A Puzzling Harvest* (Harry's *Collected Poems 1955-2000*) exemplifies the prolificacy and variety of his work, which I am sure will be remembered and will live on.

Anne Stevenson

On Line

For Harry Guest at 80

One day, on the other side of a world war,
on the other side of an ocean, I pored over mother's
bound album of tourist snapshots—England and Italy
months before I was born—then seriously said to her,
"It must have been strange to live in the olden days
when the world was black and white without any colour."
The scene flashed back on the East Coast line as I squeezed
into two tight feet of soiled upholstery. To my right,
a teen-aged nymph hunched over an iPad; in minimal clothes,
she was scrolling for fantasy shoes. Facing me,
two smart young male laptops were open for business,
closed, of course, to the window and to England
passing outside; closed again, inside, to the pressure
of eyes, flesh and feelings inches from their screens.

In the silence of clicking keys, no one looked at me
running the sharp cardboard edge of my ticket through the
uncut pages of a rare, never-read-before *Middlemarch*,
freeing trapped pockets of breath from the 19th century—
perfectly preserved and collectable, but about as compatible
with the way we live now as trilobites with kilobytes.
What a triumph of mobile technology, the four of us
spanning three centuries in the leg room of a cell,
each on a track of our own, mine certain for the terminal,
theirs heading out into cyberspace, that New World newly
opened, fully colonized already by the dazzling young.
Do they pay, maybe, with upper case Independence—I
for the luxury of lower case instant communication,
the infallible i of the pad, the pod, the impudent phone?

Summoning the shade of my mother, I said to her,
"This is how we live in the wonderland of the future."

"On a pea-sized, overpopulated planet," she answered,
"in continuous communication with itself? You're welcome to it.
And why do so many of you suffer from earache?
Are you happy living this way—not hand to mouth
but conspicuously hand to ear?" My teenage neighbour
slipped me a pitying smile as she turned off the shoes
and reached for her mobile. Outside the window I watched
four jackdaws jockey for place on a tree stripped to the bone.
They took off in a flock as we passed the aborted woodland.
Sunset. A star from a gash in the fire-coloured clouds
shone bright as an eye through our ghostly reflections.
Then night gave us all, complete in ourselves, to the glass.

Chris Ward

Harry Guest at Felsted School

Harry arrived in 1955 at Felsted School, an all-male boarding establishment in central rural Essex where he taught French, German and English Literature. It was typical of so many boarding public schools at the time—minimal personal privacy through open dormitories, showers and changing rooms. The rows of baths had no partitions and the toilets had no doors. Daily attendance at Chapel was compulsory, as was open-air exercise overseen by a marginally psychopathic retired army PT instructor. Fagging and flogging were endemic and failure to conform to the 'system' led to 'lines' or caning by a master or prefect. One required a signed *exeat* to leave the school grounds.

But within this potentially soul-destroying environment it was possible to flourish, largely through the influence of a few enlightened and liberal masters, and through music, drama and art, limited as it was at the time. Close friendships developed, some of which became lifelong.

After similar schoolboy experiences himself, and at the age of 23 at appointment, Harry was able to relate more closely to the pupils than the established masters. He had a refreshingly informal and charismatic approach to teaching which, as a boy on the sciences track, I was only aware of among the non-scientists. Their views were respected. They were encouraged to debate and challenge institutional dogma, while he himself would occasionally be able to negotiate release of boys from disproportionate or inappropriate punishment.

He was outraged by the tradition of so much compulsory sport for all, regardless of a boy's aptitude. He tried, but failed, to advocate the tailoring of out-of-class activities that boys might actually enjoy or be good at; in other words to promote a greater degree of individuality. He himself expressed his own sense of self in a small way by refusing to wear the gown of a master at any time. It was not surprising, but of no consequence to him, that he was not popular with some of his peers.

His greatest contribution to the school came outside the classroom where, unconstrained by curriculum, he could spread his wings. His arenas were the stage, the debating society, the Shakespeare society and the Andrew society which encouraged literary expression and where he could promote his passion for poetry and encourage boys to write and present their own. He put on early Pinter plays and directed innovative interpretations of Shakespeare and Reformation plays. But he was never an iconoclast. He creatively and imaginatively replaced what he might have attacked or deleted.

He was much missed when he left Felsted for Lancing in 1961 but his influence remains with those he touched. In the course of recent conversations and letters it is obvious that his wit, mischievousness, energy and inventiveness are undimmed.

www.ingramcontent.com/pod-product-compliance
Lightning Source LLC
Chambersburg PA
CBHW031154160426
43193CB00008B/356